BUILD IT! FESTIVAL

Teacher's Guide

Grades K–6
(may be adapted for Grades 7, 8, and above)

Skills
Observing, Building Models, Constructing, Communicating, Finding and Articulating Patterns, Cooperating, Predicting, Finding Multiple Solutions, Drawing Conclusions, Learning Geometric Definitions, Problem-Solving

Concepts
Shape Recognition, Polygons, Polyhedra (edges, faces, vertices), Spatial Visualization, Surface Area, Pattern, Symmetry, Congruence, Similarity, Architectural Design, Tessellations

Science Themes
Structure, Scale, Models and Simulations, Diversity and Unity

Mathematics Strands
Geometry, Logic and Language, Number, Discrete Mathematics, Functions

Nature of Science and Mathematics
Cooperative Efforts, Interdisciplinary, Real-Life Applications

by
Philip Gonsalves and Jaine Kopp

LHS GEMS

Great Explorations in Math and Science (GEMS)
Lawrence Hall of Science
University of California at Berkeley

Cover Design
Rose Craig

Illustrations
Rose Craig
Carol Bevilacqua
Lisa Klofkorn

Photographs
Richard Hoyt
Jan M. Goodman

Lawrence Hall of Science, University of California, Berkeley, CA 94720

Chairman: Glenn T. Seaborg
Director: Marian C. Diamond

Publication of *Build It! Festival* was made possible by a grant from the McDonnell-Douglas Employee's Community Fund and the McDonnell-Douglas Foundation. The GEMS Project and the Lawrence Hall of Science greatly appreciate this support.

Initial support for the origination and publication of the GEMS series was provided by the A.W. Mellon Foundation and the Carnegie Corporation of New York. Under a grant from the National Science Foundation, GEMS Leader's Workshops were held across the country. GEMS has also received support from the McDonnell-Douglas Foundation and the McDonnell-Douglas Employees Community Fund, the Hewlett Packard Company, and the people at Chevron USA. GEMS also gratefully acknowledges the contribution of word processing equipment from Apple Computer, Inc. This support does not imply responsibility for statements or views expressed in publications of the GEMS program.

For further information on GEMS leadership opportunities, or to receive a publication brochure and the *GEMS Network News*, please contact GEMS at the address below.

International Standard Book Number:
0-924886-38-2

COMMENTS WELCOME

Great Explorations in Math and Science (GEMS) is an ongoing curriculum development project. GEMS guides are revised periodically, to incorporate teacher comments and new approaches. We welcome your criticisms, suggestions, helpful hints, and any anecdotes about your experience presenting GEMS activities. Your suggestions will be reviewed each time a GEMS guide is revised. Please send your comments to:
GEMS Revisions,
c/o Lawrence Hall of Science,
University of California, Berkeley, CA 94720.
The phone number is (510) 642-7771.
The fax number is (510) 643-0309.

Great Explorations in Math and Science (GEMS) Program

The Lawrence Hall of Science (LHS) is a public science center on the University of California at Berkeley campus. LHS offers a full program of activities for the public, including workshops and classes, exhibits, films, lectures, and special events. LHS is also a center for teacher education and curriculum research and development.

Over the years, LHS staff have developed a multitude of activities, assembly programs, classes, and interactive exhibits. These programs have proven to be successful at the Hall and should be useful to schools, other science centers, museums, and community groups. A number of these guided-discovery activities have been published under the Great Explorations in Math and Science (GEMS) title, after an extensive refinement process that includes classroom testing of trial versions, modifications to ensure the use of easy-to-obtain materials, and carefully written and edited step-by-step instructions and background information to allow presentation by teachers without special background in mathematics or science.

Staff

Glenn T. Seaborg, **Principal Investigator**
Jacqueline Barber, **Director**
Kimi Hosoume, **Assistant Director**
Cary Sneider, **Curriculum Specialist**
Carolyn Willard, **GEMS Centers Coordinator**
Laura Tucker, **GEMS Workshop Coordinator**
Terry Cort, **GEMS Workshop Representative**
Katharine Barrett, Kevin Beals, Ellen Blinderman, Beatrice Boffen, Gigi Dornfest, John Erickson, Jaine Kopp, Laura Lowell, Linda Lipner, Debra Sutter, Rebecca Tilley, **Staff Development Specialists**
Jan M. Goodman, **Mathematics Consultant**
Cynthia Eaton, **Administrative Coordinator**

Karen Milligan, **Distribution Coordinator**
Felicia Roston, **Shipping Coordinator**
George Kasarjian, **Shipping Assistant**
Stephanie Van Meter, **Program Assistant**
Lisa Haderlie Baker, **Art Director**
Carol Bevilacqua, Rose Craig, Lisa Klofkorn, **Designers**
Lincoln Bergman, **Principal Editor**
Carl Babcock, **Senior Editor**
Florence Stone, **Assistant Editor**
Kay Fairwell, **Principal Publications Coordinator**
Erica De Cuir, Larry Gates, Lisa Ghahraman, Nancy Kedzierski, Alisa Sramala, Vivian Tong, Mary Yang, **Staff Assistants**

Contributing Authors

Jacqueline Barber
Katharine Barrett
Kevin Beals
Lincoln Bergman
Celia Cuomo
Linda De Lucchi
Gigi Dornfest

Jean Echols
Philip Gonsalves
Jan M. Goodman
Alan Gould
Kimi Hosoume
Susan Jagoda
Jaine Kopp

Linda Lipner
Laura Lowell
Larry Malone
Cary I. Sneider
Debra Sutter
Jennifer Meux White
Carolyn Willard

Reviewers

We would like to thank the following educators who reviewed, tested, or coordinated the reviewing of *this series* of GEMS materials in manuscript and draft form. Their critical comments and recommendations, **based on classroom presentation of these activities nation-wide**, contributed significantly to these GEMS publications. Their participation in the review process does not necessarily imply endorsement of the GEMS program or responsibility for statements or views expressed. Their role is an invaluable one, and their feedback is carefully recorded and integrated as appropriate into the publications. **THANK YOU!**

ALASKA

Wasilla, Alaska
Iditarod Elementary School
   Tacy M. Carr
   Cynthia Dolmas Curran
   Ruth Felberg
   Carol Lowery

ARKANSAS

Jonesboro, Arkansas
Coordinator: **Mark McJunkin**
Valley View Elementary School
   Faye Fowler
   Virginia Moore
   Karen Rogers
   Jane Ryals

CALIFORNIA

Huntington Beach, California
Coordinator: **Susan Spoeneman**
Daniel Webster Elementary School
   Kathryn Donley
   Doris P. Lipiz
   Ruthie H. Mendoza
   Joan Prater

San Francisco Bay Area
Coordinators: **Cynthia Ashley**
                Cynthia Eaton

Downer School, San Pablo
   Laura Olson
   Lina Prairie
   Kathleen Smallfield
   Emily Vogler
   Douglas Wheeler

Lafayette School, Lafayette
   Terese Atallah
   Linda Marsden
   Michael Meneghetti

Longfellow School, Berkeley
   Cris Barrere
   Hillary Hoppock

Malcolm X School, Berkeley
   Angela Archie
   DeEtte LaRue
   Jessie Shohara
   Gloria Thornton

John Marshall School, Oakland
   Lew Williams

Carl Munck School, Oakland
   Marka Carson
   Judy Finch
   Dorothy Hamilton
   Steven Miyamoto

Marie Murphy School, Richmond
   Debby Callahan
   Patsy Christner
   Mary Neuman
   Sandra Petzoldt

Oxford School, Berkeley
   Anita Baker
   Carolyn Dobson
   Barbara Edwards
   Jessica Vaughan

Park Day School, Oakland
   Harriet Cohen
   Karen Corzan
   Michelle Krueger

Sequoia School, Oakland
   Cindy Cathey
   Jeannie Kohl
   Barbara Schmidt
   Lisa Taymuree
   Laurie Wingate

St. Augustine School, Oakland
   Diane Dias
   Helen Raphael
   Rita Samper
   Patricia Schmitz

Steffan Manor School, Vallejo
   Don Baer
   Annie Howard
   Bridget Winkley

COLORADO

Fort Collins, Colorado
Barton Elementary School
   Alice Atencio Howe
   Valeria A. Lima
   Ted P. Stoeckley
   Judith Viola

GEORGIA

Harlem, Georgia
North Harlem Elementary School
   Linda M. Barron
   Roberta A. Gralenski
   Julie Sibilsky Simpson
   Barbara M. Watts

IDAHO

Sagle, Idaho
Sagle Elementary School
  Betty Collins
  Steve Guthrie
  Tim Hanna
  Susan E. Stevens

KENTUCKY

Louisville, Kentucky
Fern Creek Elementary School
  Ginny Gilliland
  Charlotte Nedros
  Carol Porter
  Donna J. Stevenson

MICHIGAN

Grand Blanc, Michigan
Indian Hill Elementary School
  Kent M. Brandt
  Jane L. Burgess
  Mary Ann Schloegl
  Vickie Dee Weiss

Hickory Corners, Michigan
Gull Lake Community Schools
  Gary Denton
  Stirling Fenner
  Debi Kilmartin
  Denise Rice

NORTH CAROLINA

Charlotte, North Carolina
Lake Wylie Elementary School
  Debbie Camp
  Ann Knight Thomas
  Glenda M. Nance
  Lyn Sweet

TEXAS

Decatur, Texas
Coordinator: **Shirley Watson**
Decatur Elementary School
  Carmen Antoine
  Agnes Burnett
  Lori Clark
  Carol Hale

WASHINGTON

Forks, Washington
Coordinators: **David Kennedy**,
State Superintendent of Schools
and **Sherry Schaaf**
Forks Elementary School
  Campbell Crawford
  Mary Anne McClaire
  David N. McIrvin
  Laurie Turner

Acknowledgments

Inspired by the success of the "Math-O-Rama" Festival and knowing how much students love to build, co-author Jaine Kopp came up with the idea for the "Build It! Festival" outreach program. This hands-on festival of building stations was first designed to serve entire elementary schools of kindergarten through sixth graders.

The major work of designing and creating the original stations for this festival was done by Tim Aaronson, Celia Cuomo, Rosita Fabian, Randall Fastabend, Jan Goodman, and Jaine Kopp. Since it first went to schools in the early 1990s, the "Build It! Festival" has been further evolved by every staff member who presents it, including—in addition to co-authors Philip Gonsalves and Jaine Kopp—Celia Cuomo, Randall Fastabend, Jan Goodman, and Mel McMurrin.

This learning station GEMS Teacher's Guide, which adapts the all-school event to the individual classroom, has involved the help and hard work of many people. Special thanks to the trial test teachers whose feedback helped refine and polish the activities. Their names are listed in the front of the guide. In addition, Jacquey Barber, Lincoln Bergman, Kimi Hosoume, Linda Lipner, and Carolyn Willard joined the two authors of this guide in reviewing the teacher feedback and each of the many drafts of this guide. Cynthia Ashley and Cynthia Eaton did a stellar job coordinating the local and national testing process. They were assisted by Felicia Roston who skillfully and creatively put together the materials and kits for both trials. Co-author Philip Gonsalves created the original graphics for the teaching masters in this guide. And for the "special touches" that enhance this guide, our thanks to: Lisa Klofkorn for layout and design; Lincoln Bergman for the inspired geometric poetry; Rose Craig for the gorgeous cover; and Jacquey Barber and Florence Stone for polishing the text in this geometric gem.

Our appreciation to all the students who were the builders and gave us their important feedback on our blueprints. They made many important suggestions for the refinement of the guide. We also thank the students at Downer School in San Pablo, Carl Munck School in Oakland, and Oxford School in Berkeley, who grace the photographs in this guide.

Contents

For several years, the Lawrence Hall of Science Mathematics Education Department has been very successfully taking the "Build It! Festival" outreach program to schools throughout California and Nevada, captivating large school groups with this highly popular participatory event.

At a large-group "Build It! Festival," the different activities are set up in a large room (gym or multi-purpose) and groups of students, partnered with a classmate, come in and rotate through, doing the activities. The activities utilize a variety of building materials and address many mathematical skills which students eagerly explore. Signs at the learning stations where the materials are located encourage student challenges.

For our large group festival presentations, the activities are not intended to be completed in any special order and students are free to select the activities they want to try. The only limitation is the number of people who are able to take part in an activity at any given time.

The "Build It! Festival" program has also been very well-received as the focus for Family Nights at schools, and the large group festival could also work well at after-school programs and community centers.

This GEMS Teacher's Guide adapts the large group festival to the individual classroom, but could also be used in staging your own large group event, so long as the desired number of stations and necessary quantities of materials are taken into account.

Introduction: Into the Classroom

This GEMS *Build It! Festival* Teacher's Guide was developed largely in response to many teachers expressing interest in having the activities from the large group "Build It! Festival" available for classroom use. The classroom adaptation makes use of a **learning station** format, with materials and signs set up on tables or counter tops so small groups of students can come to the station and take part in a stimulating hands-on activity that refines their skills, helps them explore mathematical concepts, connects to the real, practical world, and, at best, catalyzes their curiosity for further exploration.

Our intention in adapting "Build It! Festival" to the classroom is to make these activities useful to teachers and students in as many ways as possible. **You can decide which approach best suits your students' needs.** Please note that we have divided some activities into two options—one designed for younger students and the other for older students, without delineating exact grade levels. In these cases, select the one that best suits your students' levels and abilities.

It's also important at the start to recognize that, as one would imagine, materials that students can build with are an essential part of this unit. There are many considerations you will need to take into account with respect to quantity, price, and ways to obtain these materials. Please see the special section "Materials You Need" immediately following this introduction (page 13), and the section on "Sources for Materials," at the end of the book (page 213).

Each or all of the activities can stand on their own as exciting and "constructive" ways to involve **all** students in hands-on mathematical learning. At the same time, the activities can serve as the "groundbreaking ceremony" for an in-depth study of a particular topic, or be used in conjunction with a unit on three-dimensional geometry, or become a key "building block" of an integrated unit involving science, math, social studies, and literature.

Breaking New Ground...

Build It! Festival is sure to bring out the builder in all of your students. These open-ended and inviting activities allow for creative and practical learning about mathematics through hands-on experiences. Together, these experiences help students construct new understandings and skills, with numerous real-life connections. In your classroom you may see:

... several students working together to build a structure out of newspaper dowels, using their knowledge of shapes to make it stable;

... a student who feels unsure about his mathematical abilities successfully putting together the seven tangram shapes to make a square;

... students eagerly manipulating and investigating two- and three-dimensional figures from many angles;

... a student enjoying the beauty of tessellations and discovering that she *really is* doing mathematics;

... a classroom humming with activity as students work constructively and cooperatively;

... all of your students involved in what they are doing and learning more about geometry, shapes, and structures by building at their own pace and level.

These activities can help to break new ground, pouring in a solid, concrete foundation for your students by connecting mathematics to direct hands-on student experience and to the real world. In this way, even very young students begin to associate math with successful, creative experiences, rather than with frustration or intimidation. Doing these activities can help raise the consciousness of even the youngest students about how mathematics figures into the buildings they see around them and into numerous desirable and interesting careers. The activities, originated at the Lawrence Hall of Science and tested in classrooms nationwide, combine a high level of enjoyment and success with plenty of solid mathematical concepts and understandings.

Where's The Mathematics?

At first glance, an uninformed observer might think students were simply having lots of fun building and constructing. We know from many years of educational experience that this kind of enjoyment can be a very important ingredient in learning! In fact, *Build It! Festival* is a valuable and effective educational experience in many ways.

Each activity has **key mathematical concepts** at its core. Still, the mathematical concepts involved may not be readily apparent to someone who walks into your classroom and sees a pile of newspaper dowels being turned into a structure. What math skills could they be using? As they create a base, students are using **triangles** to give the structure stability. Another group is making a model of a **tetrahedron**. They are examining **angles** and sides of **shapes** and much math goes into the building. Younger students may just be fitting the dowels together with a hit-or-miss method—and that is fine too! They are gaining hands-on experience that contributes to an intuitive understanding of **shape** and its relationship to **structure** which can be further applied when they encounter three-dimensional shapes again.

Build It! Festival has **geometry** as its foundation, and other areas of mathematics as the beams, of a structure that can be completed by adding other curricula and skills. Woven throughout the guide are opportunities for students to reinforce their knowledge of **geometric figures**. Through direct experience, they become aware of the properties and relationship of **polygons** and **polyhedra** and are able to analyze and manipulate shapes. With this knowledge, students can then begin to look for **patterns** and **designs** in the world around them. Tilings open the door to the world of **tessellations** and **symmetry** which can evolve from an exploration of design. Along the path, students develop **spatial sense**.

As students are busy filling a shape different ways with pattern blocks, they are building several **models** of a single polygon. Through this manipulation of pattern block shapes, students not only develop spatial sense but also can begin to explore the concept of **substitution**, which is a form of **equivalence**—a skill later utilized in **algebra**. Likewise, they are developing **number sense**. Students can also delve into explorations of the **areas** and **perimeters** of the polygons they fill. In this way, even in a single seemingly simple activity, a wealth of mathematical learning takes place as students work cooperatively and share their solutions.

Vocabulary will naturally grow as students proceed through the stations. **While we have included a Geometric Glossary in the "Behind the Scenes" section (page 193), the emphasis is most definitely NOT on vocabulary but, as in all GEMS guides, on "learning by doing."**

What your students will gain from this unit varies depending upon their ages, experience, and abilities. If at one station an older student might have the opportunity to learn about such concepts as **congruence** and **similarity of shapes**, that does not necessarily mean that a first grader should be expected to gain awareness of these concepts at that station. Younger students will gain memorable practical experiences and intuitive understandings which can be called upon when they encounter these ideas again in upper grades.

From start to finish, and at all points in between, *Build It! Festival* is literally filled with mathematics!

Presenting *Build-It!* To Your Students

Stations and Activities

In the guide we refer to both **activities** and **stations**. The *activities* **are what the students do** (such as using pattern blocks to fill shapes in the Fill-A-Shape activity). The *stations* **(or *learning stations*) are the physical locations where the students carry out the activity**. For example, your entire class can be working on the Fill-A-Shape activity at six learning stations in the classroom. Each station will probably have six students at it (more or less depending upon your classroom situation). Working at stations with others, students gain important cooperative skills, and having different small groups working at the same station often allows students to more readily see and comprehend **multiple solutions** to the activity.

A "learning station" is a classroom table, cluster of desks, or counter top set up with equipment or materials designed to encourage students to make their own discoveries. The class participates in open-ended exploration in an informal, student-centered way. (Another term many teachers use for this format is "learning centers.")

Formats

Depending upon your own preferences and teaching style, the background and experience of your students, and the physical layout of your classroom, you may wish to use one particular format for your classroom festival or you may want to combine the activities and stations in your own way. All formats rely on learning stations in the classroom; they differ in respect to whether or not there are one or more activities set up at those learning stations.

WHOLE CLASS STATION FORMAT:
From the collective experience of teachers, the Whole Class Station Format is strongly recommended as the most successful format to **initially** present *Build-It! Festival*. This format first introduces the entire class to the activity and then all students explore that same activity in pairs or small groups at learning stations during a class period. This method familiarizes students with the materials and the initial task at the station. As students are working, you are free to circulate to observe, assist, and ask questions as appropriate to encourage more student investigation. The optional signs at the stations can also encourage students to "go further" with each activity. This format can also make the activity "debriefing" rich with student

When you introduce or demonstrate activities, if possible use an area in the classroom set aside for group discussion, separate from the stations where students will work with the materials. If this is not possible in your setting, wait until after you have presented the introduction or demonstration before you give out the materials.

We are sometimes asked to recommend the "pedagogically correct" sequence for these activities. There is no "right answer" to that question. In fact, there are multiple solutions! The sequence depends on prior student experience as well as expected learning outcomes. For example, many teachers use Build It! Festival *as an entry into the world of geometry. For this purpose, you could begin with activities involving two-dimensional shapes. After free exploration of pattern blocks and the Architect/Builder activity, one appropriate sequence would be: Fill-A-Shape/ What Comes Next?/ Tessellations/ Symmetry/ Tangrams. Both What Comes Next? and Tessellations involve pattern—an underlying theme of mathematics at all grade levels. What Comes Next? provides opportunities to explore sequential, numeric, and geometric patterns while Tessellations extends pattern to the entire plane. Symmetry can be challenging for many students, therefore, presenting it after the pattern-related activities helps foster more positive experiences. The Tangrams activity reinforces and extends the concept of polygons while introducing additional geometric concepts such as congruence and similarity. Then, based on experiences with two-dimensional shapes, students are more prepared for three-dimensional activities. Of these, Dowel Designs is the most accessible. It allows students to build in two and three dimensions, in both open-ended and more directed ways. Then either Create-A-Shape or Polyhedra provide concrete models to connect the structures built in Dowel Designs with defined three-dimensional geometric shapes.* **Please understand that this sequence is just one suggestion—there are other excellent variations that build from two- to three-dimensional shapes.**

discoveries. After this initial class session, a learning station (or learning center) with the activity readied on it, can be set up in one place in the classroom, so that students can revisit it for further investigations.

SINGLE STATION FORMAT: Some teachers have used a Single Station Format as a part of an on-going series of mathematics learning stations. They set up one activity at a single learning station in their classrooms and have small group(s) of students work there during the regular math class period or any other appropriate class time. You can either introduce the activity— especially for younger students—or, with older students, send them to the stations, have them follow the station's directions, and make their own mathematical discoveries!

DIVERSE STATION FORMAT: The Diverse Station Format is another way to present *Build It! Festival* to the whole class, similar to the way the large-group all-school festival is conducted. In this format, learning stations with diverse activities are set up around the room and students circulate through them with a partner. You could have a different activity at each learning station. Or you could have, for example, six stations altogether, with the same activity at several of them—for example, two stations with the Fill-A-Shape activity, two stations with the Create-A-Shape activity, and two stations with the Symmetry activity. The stations might be set up in the classroom for at least two different math periods of about 45 minutes each. **Many teachers use the Diverse Station Format after they have introduced all the activities individually to their classes in the Whole Class Station Format. Students can then return to favorite activities to consolidate their knowledge and to make new discoveries.**

Planning the Sequence of the Activities

Although students go through the activities in any order they choose at large-group festivals, teachers who use these activities in classrooms tend to sequence them in ways that they prefer, **often differently from the order in which they appear in this guide.** The amount of time teachers devote to each activity also varies, as, of course, does the way the activities are combined with mathematics topics and integrated across the curriculum.

Some teachers may want to emphasize particular concepts in geometry, or use one activity as a springboard to a larger unit, or may decide that another order makes more logical pedagogical sense for their students. **This is fine—there is no one correct way to order these activities, and we're sure that you will come up with your own creative adaptations.**

Here are samples of sequences that could be used to present a festival in your classroom. Feel free to come up with your own!

Time Frame Considerations

The time needed to present *Build It! Festival* depends of course in large part on the choices you make regarding format and sequences. It also depends on your own preferences and the specific needs and abilities of your students.

For example, you could do a "Mini Three-Dimensional Unit," such as the following, over a two week period:

Day 1: Free Exploration of the polyhedra building materials (snap-together triangles, squares, and pentagons).

Day 2: Vocabulary Development of Polyhedra with an activity that uses the vocabulary, such as sorting polyhedra by the number of faces (or edges or vertices).

Day 3: Create-A-Shape Activity for students to build models of three-dimensional shapes. Students review vocabulary.

Day 4: Choose an extension activity from Create-A-Shape appropriate to your students.

Day 5: Introduce Dowel Designs. Have all students freely construct with dowels.

Day 6: Directed Building with Dowels, such as comparing and contrasting tetrahedrons and pyramids.

Fill-A-Shape
What Comes Next?
Symmetry
Create-A-Shape
Tessellations
Tangrams

Architect/Builder
What Comes Next?
Tangrams
Fill-A-Shape
Symmetry
Dowel Designs

A Mini Three-Dimensional Unit
Polyhedra
Create-A-Shape
Dowel Designs

Architect/Builder
What Comes Next?
Tessellations
Fill-A-Shape
Symmetry
Tangrams

Architect/Builder
Fill-A-Shape
Symmetry
Tangrams
Polyhedra
Dowel Designs

Diverse Station Format Sequences
Day 1: Create-A-Shape, Polyhedra, Symmetry
Day 2: Fill-A-Shape, Tangrams, What Comes Next?
Day 3: Dowel Designs, Tessellations

Due to the high interest level of Dowel Designs, we recommend having many stations of this activity so that all students will have an opportunity to do it.

Day 7: Build a three-dimensional polyhedron with toothpicks and peas. Have students write descriptions to define their shapes.

Day 8: Have each of the three activities at separate learning stations so that students can revisit them.

Day 9: Create a building and then a city! Have students each make a model of the Building Master and then create other buildings and structures that are in a city. Combine buildings to make a city. Add proportionally sized roads, driveways, cars, people, etc.

Day 10: Continue the city-building project.

In addition, during this mini unit, you might be able to arrange a field trip to a construction site to observe the skeleton of a building. Depending on the interest of your students, you may want to continue the unit with some of the "Going Further" activities or you could use them as homework assignments.

A different approach to scheduling the festival would be to present it over an eight week period. Each week you could introduce one of the activities to the entire class. For the remainder of that week, you could choose which "Going Further" activities you would like students to explore. Additionally, you could set up a learning station with the activity of the week for students to revisit at appropriate class times.

Still another way to schedule the festival in your classroom would be to present activities in a variety of ways over the course of one week. For example, on the first day, have learning stations available with pattern blocks. Develop a geometric vocabulary for the blocks and have students make discoveries. Students can record their findings in journals. On the next day, do the Architect/Builder activity with the class. Then for the next two days, set up learning stations with pattern block activities and let students rotate through the learning stations. After going to the learning stations each day, students can write one thing that they learned at a station in their journals. On the final day, have the students create a set of tangrams to explore another set of polygons. Students can compare the tangram shapes to the pattern blocks and then use the tangrams for geometric discoveries appropriate to their abilities.

These are just three *possible* ways to schedule the festival in your classroom. The beauty of this guide is that you can mix and match activities and the amount of time you spend on them according to your interests and those of your students. We encourage you to "build" your own unique festival!

"Blueprint" for the *Build It! Festival* Guide

This *Build It! Festival* GEMS Teacher's Guide contains a very important preliminary activity, an introductory activity, eight main learning station activities, as well as some intriguing extension ideas.

Before you present any of the activities to your students, we strongly recommend that you present the preliminary and introductory activities. The first, **Free Exploration**, is a very open-ended activity designed to encourage exactly what its name implies. The other, **Architect/Builder**, is more structured. We designed these activities to both introduce your students to pattern blocks— one of the main materials used in the Festival—and to whet their appetites for more.

From Free Exploration and Architect/Builder, your students then move on to some or all of the following: Create-A-Shape; Dowel Designs; Polyhedra; Fill-A-Shape; Symmetry; What Comes Next?; Tessellations; and Tangrams. These eight main learning station activities each include the following sections:

1. An **"Overview"** that briefly explains the activity and in some cases gives background information.

2. A **"What You Need"** section that lists the materials that you need for each station. **The materials listed are the estimated amounts to accommodate six students at each station, and a class of about 32 students in all. If you will have more than six students at a station at any one time, you will need to adjust the amount of materials accordingly. (See also the special**

section on materials and signs that immediately follows this "Introduction," and the "Sources for Materials" on page 213.)

3. The **"Getting Ready"** section tells you how to prepare the materials and the signs for each station. The signs are listed as optional, in case your students do not read, or if you decide to do only an opening demonstration/explanation of the activity without later use of the signs. Occasionally, you may need to present a preliminary activity to prepare your students for the station and this section alerts you to this. It also alerts you to the need to gather materials for the presentation.

4. A **"Special Considerations"** section provides tips on how to best implement the station, possible pitfalls to avoid, and suggestions for preliminary activities for the students that relate to the main activity. **Please be sure to read this section before presenting the activities.**

5. The **"Presenting/Doing the Activity"** section, which explains how to present the activity, what the students will be doing, lists sample questions to pose, and/or notes things to observe in students' work.

6. The **"Going Further"** section suggests ways to extend the activity, as part of an on-going math program and across the curriculum, or to delve more deeply into an aspect of the activity. We have attempted to list a range of "Going Further" activities to span the kindergarten through sixth grade range.

We have also provided some additional information for teachers. The **"Behind the Scenes"** section on geometry is intended for teachers to use as a reference and background. This is intended for your use; it is **not** meant to be read out loud to students, nor is it in any way our intention that students learn or memorize the information in it...nor should you! On the contrary, the essence of these activities is direct student experience and experimentation, providing the start of a solid foundation for introduction of more abstract concepts much later on in their academic growth.

The **"Resource Books"** and **"Literature Connections"** sections list a number of books (in addition to those referred to more directly in the activity write-ups) that support and extend the concepts embodied in the activities. We welcome your additional suggestions, including non-fiction resources for this age group, as well as young people's storybooks and literature that reflect the mathematical and building-related content of *Build It! Festival.*

Building On *Build It!*

This teacher's guide seeks to provide sufficient information for you to successfully bring out the creative builder in all of your students. As always, we welcome your comments and suggestions. All GEMS guides are revised frequently, based on your comments and suggestions.

Build It! Festival provides a solid foundation for delving deeper. Let the enthusiasm from the Festival carry you and your students into further explorations. Many suggestions that range across the curriculum are provided throughout the guide—from origami paper airplanes/aerodynamics, art and creative writing, and the numerous other ideas we suggest to your own creative ways to extend this festival unit.

On whatever paths *Build It! Festival* may take you, you can be sure that you and your students will gain a new perspective on what mathematics can encompass and how central a role it plays in building and changing our world. Build on!

Materials You Need

Please see the "Sources for Materials" section on page 213 for specific ordering information from a variety of sources.

PATTERN BLOCKS

We thought long and hard about what manipulatives to use at this Festival. For many reasons, we decided to use pattern blocks as a main manipulative. One of the most important reasons being their appeal to students. Many teachers report that in their classrooms, students often choose these brightly-colored geometric shapes during free choice work periods. At this Festival, pattern blocks are used in four of the eight regular activities as well as for the preliminary and introductory activities.

Students use the pattern blocks to gain insights into many aspects of geometry as well as pattern and number. The pattern blocks also lend themselves to artist creations tying mathematics with visual arts. But this just scratches the surface of the power of pattern blocks as a mathematical teaching tool. To name a few, they can be used to teach number concepts such as addition, multiplication, and fractions; as a non-standard tool for measurement; as a tool for expressing functions and algebraic expressions; and as a concrete material to explore discrete mathematics.

Pattern blocks are available in wood or plastic. We highly recommend the wooden blocks because they can also be used to create three-dimensional structures. Another variety of pattern blocks is a set of elaborate plastic rainbow pattern blocks featuring the six shapes in six different vibrant colors. Because these are thicker, they, like wooden blocks, can be used to build three-dimensionally. There is also a giant-sized set of carpet tile pattern blocks available which is ideal for modeling and for young students to use to build.

To present the pattern block activities to a class of 32 students, we recommend that you have at least six sets of 250 pattern blocks or four sets of 432 pattern blocks. If you need to acquire these, it will cost you over $100. We have tried to create pattern block task cards that use the blocks efficiently. However, for some activities, such as Tessellations, more blocks may be needed, if the entire class does the activity at the same time. If this much expense exceeds your abilities, you can still use the learning station activities in this book which require pattern blocks by ordering only one or two sets and using either the Single Station Format or the Diverse Station Format. **We know some teachers, who, if they had to choose only one math manipulative for their classrooms, would choose pattern blocks!**

POLYHEDRA

The materials needed for the Polyhedra activity are expensive, **but** this activity is so popular with everyone that we could not bear to leave it out! Working with polyhedra invites students to learn about three-dimensional geometry by creating shapes with flat, snap-together plastic triangles, squares, and pentagons. Students have fun creating their own imaginative shapes and then focus on the geometry involved. If you do not already have or have access to polyhedra, you will need to spend approximately $90 for the polyhedra at one learning station. **To help alleviate the cost of this material, some schools have designated a portion of the school's materials budget to acquire a school set. The polyhedra can then be shared by classrooms or used for a math lab.**

ACTIVITY CARDS

Many of the activities have student activity cards to accompany them. These are on Duplicating Masters within each of the activities and are meant to be duplicated on card stock for durability. In many cases, these cards are labeled "A," "B," and "C" to designate order of difficulty with "A" being the easiest and "C" being the most challenging. The guide is spiral bound for your copying convenience.

PAPER MATERIALS

Newspaper: One of the activities, Dowel Designs, uses newspaper as its main material. This enables students to help contribute to the Festival and encourages creative reuse of materials.

Card Stock: As noted above, many of the activities have activity cards that go with them. These cards need to be made one time and for greater durability we recommend card stock. We also recommend that you use **white** card stock so that the colors of the pattern blocks will stand out.

Colored Paper for Duplication: The Tangrams activity uses square sheets of paper or regular 8 ½" x 11" sheets to duplicate a master. We recommend using a variety of colors for this activity, so that at the stations, each student will have a square sheet of paper or master sheet in a color different than the others at her table. When students use the seven tangram shapes they will have distinct sets.

SIGNS

There is a sign to accompany each activity to guide students into their investigations at each station. Depending upon how you present the Festival, you may choose not to make them. Each activity has a suggested introduction that can include the explanation of what is on the sign. However, many teachers have found it helpful to have the signs to remind students of their task and to pose additional questions. When more than one activity is being presented at a time, the signs are very helpful. For many activities, we have pro-vided alternate signs for younger students. In general, the signs have a minimum of words—though beware students are often too busy building to read them!

How to Make Signs

Duplicate the master signs following each activity you have selected and laminate them onto file folders for greater durability. You will want one sign for each station for each activity.

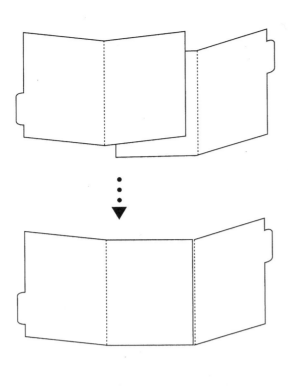

☛ Make Signs: If you do not have access to a laminator, you can use clear contact paper to cover both sides of the sign (see Step #5 below) but lamination is recommended.

1. Glue two folders together so that you have a three-panel sign backing. (Use any paper glue.)

2. Use rubber cement (it's best because the pages won't "bubble up" off the file folders) to attach duplicated signs to the backing.

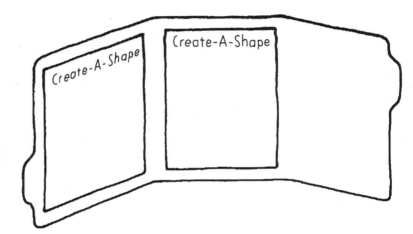

3. Laminate signs.

4. Label a tab or edge of the sign for easy retrieval from your *Build-It! Festival* file.

5. Cover the front of the sign so that the contact paper seam is not on the bottom edge of the sign. Make the contact paper a little longer than the sign and fold it up around the bottom edge.

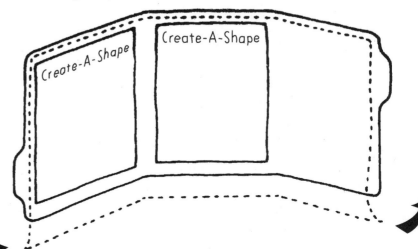

Additional Materials

Many of the additional materials that are needed are those commonly found in classrooms, such as scissors, pencils, colored pens, scotch tape, rulers, paper clips, and masking tape. Another item to be purchased is **plastic straws** for Dowel Designs. **Small mirrors** are an optional item for Symmetry. Students may be able to contribute to the materials needed. Before the Festival, you may want to send home a letter asking for assistance with materials from families.

Please see "Sources For Materials" on page 213 for specific ordering information.

Preliminary Activity: Free Exploration First!

Before using any of the manipulatives in directed activities, students need time to freely explore them. The manipulatives are of high interest and, first and foremost, students need to play and interact with them! This is of course highly educational in itself. It will also help them focus on the materials as learning tools later on, when doing more directed activities.

It is up to you to decide which materials to introduce, and in which ways. **Free exploration is extremely important**. The amount of time you choose to spend on it is variable. Some teachers introduce a new material with the entire class for one period and then have it available at a learning station or stations or as a free choice for a week before using it as a learning tool. Others only spend part of a period to explore the material and then dive into an introductory activity. The age and abilities of your students will help you decide what is appropriate for them. Your students' interest and ability to use the material in new and different ways can help guide you in evaluating how long they need to explore.

In this process of free exploration, students have opportunities to make discoveries about the manipulatives—and many of these discoveries will be mathematical! For example, students may sort by shape and color, compare size, measure, use balance to make structures, create equivalent shapes, count, or make patterns and designs.

Depending upon the age and experience of your students, the things they create will vary. Young kindergarteners may choose to stack yellow hexagons. Third graders may choose to make hexagons using triangles, parallelograms, and trapezoids. Sixth graders may create intricate symmetrical designs. Equally possible are explorations that are connected to the real world, such as using the blocks to make cities, people, space vehicles, animals, etc.

As they build, students share materials, express ideas, and learn from other students. They are also able to satisfy their curiosity. Most important is that everyone is successful—there are no right or wrong answers. In fact, there are many possible directions and by observing each others' work, students can experience the variety of possibilities.

As students are engaged in free exploration, you can use this valuable time to informally assess the skills your students already have. Throughout all the Festival activities, at all the learning stations, your observations of your students' interactions, structures, and problem-solving abilities can provide an excellent basis for assessment. Among things you may want to look for are:

- the complexity of the task that students set for themselves;
- their reactions to challenging tasks;
- how students interact with each other;
- the language that the students use;
- the interests that your students have; and
- the math skills they are using and developing.

After their initial free exploration, give students an opportunity to walk around to observe what their classmates have created. Ask for student observations and comments. List their discoveries. Ask if there were any limitations. Generate appropriate vocabulary about the manipulative.

Teachers have told us that during free exploration they observed student growth in such areas as: knowledge of geometric shapes, pattern skills, spatial sense, independent thinking skills, creativity, and understanding of equivalence and symmetry.

Introductory Activity: Architect/Builder

Overview

In this activity, pairs of students take turns being architects and builders as they design and build structures using pattern blocks. Students develop spatial concepts as the "architect" designs a structure and then gives directions to the "builder." The builder visualizes the structure and uses the spatial relationship descriptions to build the structure.

Cooperation is key to the success of this activity. It also creates a need for students to develop and practice important geometric vocabulary that will be used throughout this unit. As students describe and build, they are honing their articulation and listening skills. This activity also prepares students for the four other activities in *Build It! Festival* that use pattern blocks.

What You Need

For the teacher demonstration:
- ❒ 6–12 pattern blocks (include 1 or 2 each of the 6 shapes)
- ❒ 1 manila folder (or hard-bound book)
- ❒ 1 large sheet of butcher paper and colored markers, or an overhead projector, with transparency and transparency markers
- ❒ *(optional)* 6 large carpet tiles in the 6 pattern block shapes (See "Sources for Materials" on page 213.)

For each pair of students:
- ❒ pattern blocks (See "Getting Ready," page 24)
- ❒ containers for the blocks
- ❒ 1 manila folder (or hard-bound book)

Getting Ready

1. For each pair of younger students, place pattern blocks in containers, with two of every block in the container. There will be 12 pattern blocks—two green triangles, two orange squares, two blue parallelograms, two tan parallelograms, two red trapezoids, and two yellow hexagons—in the container. The number of blocks you use depends on the level of your students. For example, for kindergarten students, decrease the total number of blocks in the container to six—two green triangles, two orange squares, and two yellow hexagons—so that each child has one each of the three blocks. Some teachers of older students simply place a small pile of blocks (25–50) on each table for pairs of students to share.

2. Decide in advance how you will pair students for the activity (random selection, your assignment, or students choose their own partners).

3. If you are able to hold the introductory discussion away from the learning stations, you can place pattern blocks in containers or in small piles at each station for when students go to do the activity. If you do not have a separate area, prepare the blocks in containers in a central location and have one student in each pair take a container **after** the introduction.

Describing the Blocks

1. Hold up the pattern block shapes, one by one, and ask students to tell you what they know about each shape.

2. Begin with the triangle. After someone names the shape, ask students how they know it is a triangle. Encourage them to describe its characteristics. This will allow students to help create a definition for each shape. Give additional information as necessary to fully describe and define the shape. Record each shape with a picture, its color, and name. This can serve as a reference for future activities.

3. Next hold up a square. Often students will say that it is a square because it has four sides. Draw quadrilaterals that do *not* have four *equal* sides, such as the ones shown.

You may want to record on the chalkboard, a large sheet of butcher paper, or an overhead transparency for a permanent record. Some teachers have also used the pattern block tile carpets as they record each shape.

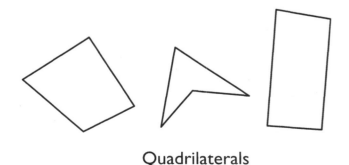

Quadrilaterals

Ask if these are squares. Students may then suggest that a square has four equal sides. Draw a parallelogram with four equal sides that is not a square.

Parallelogram

Is it a square? Why or why not? Continue the description according to your students' abilities and create a working definition for a square.

4. Hold up another pattern block, going from the more familiar to the less common shapes. Draw each shape, then record both its color and name. This will give the students several ways to identify the shapes. The list might be as follows:

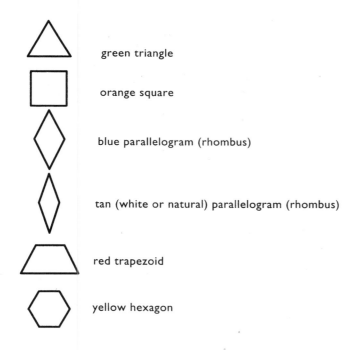

green triangle

orange square

blue parallelogram (rhombus)

tan (white or natural) parallelogram (rhombus)

red trapezoid

yellow hexagon

The blue and tan parallelograms are commonly known as diamonds and many students identify them in this way. Acknowledge this common name, then give students the geometric name for this shape— parallelogram (or rhombus). Young students enjoy learning the geometric vocabulary for shapes!

5. Older students may use more sophisticated names for shapes. They may refer to any of the four-sided shapes as a quadrilateral. As appropriate, you may want to introduce additional concepts or vocabulary appropriate for your students.

Modeling the Activity

1. Distribute one container of pattern blocks to each pair of students at desks or have students gather the containers from a central location. Alternately, distribute pattern blocks in small piles on the tables where groups are working.

2. Model the activity by taking the role of the architect and having all the students become builders. Behind a manila folder that will serve as a screen, make a simple structure, using 3–6 pattern blocks, that is appropriate to your students' abilities.

3. Tell the students that you are an architect and have designed a building that you want them to construct. (Be sure they know what an architect is!) Explain that their goal is to build a structure just like yours, according to your instructions. The challenging part is that they cannot look at the structure you've built!

4. Tell them which building materials (pattern blocks) they will need to build your structure. For example, tell them that the structure you have designed requires the following building materials: one green triangle, two red trapezoids, and one yellow hexagon.

5. Describe the construction of the structure. As you give directions, be sure that all students have completed each step before going on to the next. Explain that, *for now*, builders cannot ask questions of the architect, and must follow the directions as carefully as possible.

6. Model the task by giving as many careful and detailed directions as possible to assist the students in this process. For example, using the materials listed earlier, you can describe the illustrated structure as follows:

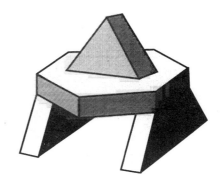

- The structure stands vertically.

- It has two red trapezoids as its base.

- The red trapezoids have their longest sides touching the table.

- They are vertical.

- The trapezoids are parallel to each other. They are like train tracks that will never meet.

- You cannot see the faces of the trapezoids.

- On top of the trapezoids, place one yellow hexagon. It is in a horizontal or flat position. An angle comes out toward you the way it is situated on top of the trapezoids.

- What shape is left? (Students often like to guess where to put this last shape. After they do, have them listen to where your green triangle is to see if it is correctly placed.)

- The green triangle is on top of the yellow hexagon. It is in a vertical position. You can tell that it is a triangle because its face is facing you.

7. After the students have completed building their structures, remove your screen and let students compare their structures to yours. Discuss questions that may arise.

8. Ask the students which words or descriptions were particularly helpful to them as you gave directions. If appropriate, list some of these words, especially those that relate to spatial relationships—vertical, horizontal, on top of, below, next to, parallel to, perpendicular, etc.—so students can use them as they become architects and builders.

Becoming Architects and Builders

1. Explain to your students that they will now do the same activity with a partner, so they have a chance to become architects and builders.

2. Explain the following points:

a. In each pair, one person will be the architect first and the other person will be the builder. After each turn, they will trade roles. Tell them they should decide who will be the architect first.

b. The architect should use an agreed-upon number of blocks to build a structure **behind a folder or book**. Her job is to describe that structure to the builder. Just as you modeled with them, the builder follows the architect's instructions to build the structure without seeing it, though the *architect does look at the builder's structure* as it is being built. As the builder works, the architect may give instructions to correct the builder, such as "You need to fix the orange square. It goes vertically—like a telephone pole."

c. The partners' goal is to work cooperatively so that both structures are the same. The architect continues to describe the structure until her partner has accurately built it. As in your demonstration, the builder is not allowed to ask any questions at this time. (As one of the "Going Further" suggestions, questions *are* allowed.)

d. After one structure is built, the partners reverse roles.

3. Distribute one manila folder (or a hard-bound book) to each pair of students, to use as the screen. Have students begin. Circulate as they work and assist students as necessary.

4. At the end of the activity, see if students want to add any additional words to the list of building terms. Then take a survey to see if students had a preference in roles. If so, why? Was one role more challenging than the other? Why?

Going Further

On subsequent days, if interest remains high, you may want to present the following variations of Architect/Builder to your students. We recommend presenting only one new version on a given day.

1. Have the architect build a structure with a few pattern blocks. In this version, it is the builder who asks questions so that she can build the structure. The architect can only answer questions with a "Yes" or "No" response. After the students are successful with this process, they can increase the number of pattern blocks according to their skill level.

2. For a greater challenge, students can include writing in this activity. Have each student build a structure with a few pattern blocks. Then, each student writes the building directions for his structure. Students exchange their directions and build each others' structures.

3. Some teachers of older students have the builder build behind a screen as the architect describes how to build the structure she designed. This provides a greater challenge for the architect—she cannot see what her partner is building until the structure is complete!

Number of Blocks
The number of pattern blocks used in this activity depends upon grade level and prior experience. For example, after several sessions of "free exploring" with the blocks, kindergarten students will be ready to begin with three or four blocks at a time while students in fourth grade may begin with six blocks after one period of free exploring. As students progress, more blocks and greater challenges can be added.

Activity 1: Create-A-Shape

Overview

Can you visualize the flat shape of a cereal box before it was folded into a box and filled? This activity invites students to investigate dimension and structure. Using two-dimensional paper shapes, students explore the construction of three-dimensional shapes.

Students start by selecting a template pattern. They predict what three-dimensional shape might be formed when the two-dimensional pattern is cut out and folded along the dotted lines. To make their own pattern, students draw around the shape using the template, cut it out, then draw in the dotted lines onto their flat shape to match those on the template. Students test their predictions by folding on the dotted lines and thus construct a three-dimensional shape! They can give their three-dimensional shapes a personal flair by decorating the faces with designs and color.

This activity helps students learn the names and attributes of three-dimensional shapes. Students can explore the number of faces and vertices. They can compare and contrast two different three-dimensional shapes. For example, examining the tetrahedron and the pyramid, students can discover that they both have four triangular faces. However, the pyramid also has a square base as its fifth face. These shapes serve as introductory, concrete models for students as they continue to develop three-dimensional geometric vocabulary and understanding.

See the section on three-dimensional shapes in the "Behind the Scenes" section on page 193 for more information on the names, attributes, and definitions of these three-dimensional shapes.

Set this activity up at one or more stations and let students explore at their own pace *or* follow the steps which begin on page 33 to introduce the activity to the entire class prior to having them work at the stations.

What You Need For One Station

❐ 6 "Create-A-Shape" templates (masters pages 39–44)
❐ 6 pairs of scissors
❐ 6 pencils and rulers
❐ 6–12 sheets of construction paper
❐ card stock on which to duplicate templates
❐ (optional) 1 Create-A-Shape sign
❐ (optional) 1 roll of scotch tape
❐ (optional) 12 markers (crayons, colored pencils)

For the teacher demonstration:

❐ 1 large piece of construction paper to make model pyramid
❐ pair of scissors
❐ 1 large sheet of butcher paper and colored markers, or an overhead projector, with transparency and transparency markers

Although any paper can be used to make the three-dimensional shapes, we strongly recommend a sturdier paper, such as construction paper, so the shapes hold up longer.

Getting Ready

1. Decide how many stations of Create-A-Shape you intend to set up.

2. Decide how many three-dimensional shape template patterns on pages 39–44 you will use with your class. Duplicate an appropriate number of templates on card stock and cut them out.

3. If you are using signs, duplicate one Create-A-Shape sign from pages 37 and 38 for each station.

4. Set up one or more Create-A-Shape learning stations around the room equipped with the materials listed in the "What You Need" section.

5. Make a large paper pyramid in the same shape as the pyramid template. Do not tape the pyramid together as you will be using it to model the process.

Some teachers have found it helpful to duplicate each shape template on a different color of card stock. Teachers have also enlisted the help of parents and/or students to cut out the shape templates.

Special Considerations

Younger students who have a limited amount of experience with drawing around a shape, cutting it out, and paper folding, may need some assistance with this activity. An older student or adult can encourage and assist them as necessary.

Start kindergarten and first grade students with the two pyramid templates labeled with an "A." They can focus on the names and number of the faces on each shape. When they are familiar with these two shapes, have them compare and contrast them.

For students beyond first grade, we recommend that you have them start with the pyramids first and work their way up through all the levels of templates from "A" through "C." Older students can also explore the number of vertices and/or edges on each three-dimensional shape.

Introducing Create-A-Shape to the Entire Class

1. Hold up the pyramid you have made. Ask students to name things they have seen with a similar shape. [The Pyramids in Egypt, tops/shapes of buildings, blocks] Next, hold the pyramid so they can see one of the triangular faces. Ask what shape it is. How many triangular faces does the pyramid have? Are there any other faces? What shape is it? [Square] In all, how many "faces" are there on the pyramid? [Five] Count the faces together to be sure everyone agrees.

2. Have students imagine what the pyramid would look like if it were opened into one flat shape with all the square faces laying flat, attached, and visible. This is a challenging spatial visualization!

3. Open the paper pyramid and let the students observe the shape. Count the triangular and square faces on the opened pyramid.

You may want to define a "face" as any one of the outside surfaces of a solid figure. The pyramid has four triangular faces and one square face. Similarily you may want to define a vertex as the point of intersection of two sides of an angle.

We recommend against taping the shapes at this time. Taping is of course one option, but not taping allows them to be folded and unfolded several times so more observations can be made. They can then also be carried home open and make neat puzzles for children to share with their parents and siblings. If students want to, they can tape their shapes at home. (Also, not taping now means one less class material for you to get together!)

You may want to record on the chalkboard, a large sheet of butcher paper, or an overhead transparency for a permanent record.

4. Explain to the students that they are going to be creating three-dimensional shapes out of paper. Hold up the template for the pyramid that matches the one you have made. Model how to create a shape:

a. Draw around the template shape onto a sheet of paper.

b. Cut out the shape.

c. Copy the dotted lines onto the shape. (This can be done freehand or with a ruler.)

d. Fold along the dotted lines to create the triangular faces.

e. Form the pyramid!

f. Decorate the pyramid, if you wish.

5. Tell students that there are templates at each station to create three-dimensional shapes. Before they get started with a template, ask them to predict what shape they think the template will create.

6. Have students go to stations. Circulate as they are working, and assist students as needed, especially in drawing the dotted lines. Ask focusing questions such as:

- "How many faces does your three-dimensional shape have?"

- "What are the shapes of the faces?"

- "How many vertices does your shape have?"

7. Make a chart of the three-dimensional shapes with your class to record findings. Include a picture of the shape, its name, and the other geometric information appropriate to your students such as the number of faces, edges, and vertices. Older students may also want to record this in their math journals.

8. After students have created more than one shape, have them compare and contrast two shapes. Ask probing questions such as:

- Do the shapes have the same number of faces?

- Do the shapes have similar faces—for example, do they both have triangular faces?

- Does one shape have more vertices than the other?

Going Further

1. **"Feel-y Box" 3-D Geometry**: Using just their sense of touch, have students reach into a "feel-y box" and guess what shape is in it. You may want to have pictures of the possible shapes to help students identify what they are feeling. Alternately, have a student describe a shape to the class and see if students can visualize and guess the shape!

2. **Have a "Boxtravaganza!"** Have students bring in boxes from home. Find out how many faces there are on each box and identify the shapes of the faces. Predict what the box will look like as a two-dimensional shape. Students could record their predictions on paper or in journals. Cut the box to form **one** flat shape. (You may need to cut off extraneous inside flaps to avoid confusion about the main box shape.) How many different ways can you cut the box to create a two-dimensional shape? What is the longest shape you can make? The shortest? For young students a wonderful book to read along with this box activity is *My Cat Likes to Hide in Boxes*.

3. **Create a Museum of Three-Dimensional Shapes!** Have students bring in three-dimensional shapes from home. Label the shapes. (See the Geometric Glossary in "Behind the Scenes" on page 193.) Have students sort and classify the shapes in a variety of ways, such as those with square bases or by the number of faces on the shape.

4. **Paper Jackets for Shapes**: Have students make "jackets" for solid three-dimensional shapes that will fit over the shape exactly. Compare the sizes and shapes of the jackets. Older students can use grid paper and investigate surface area.

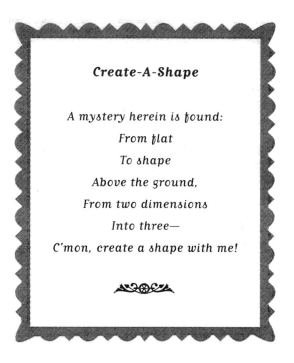

Create-A-Shape

A mystery herein is found:
From flat
To shape
Above the ground,
From two dimensions
Into three—
C'mon, create a shape with me!

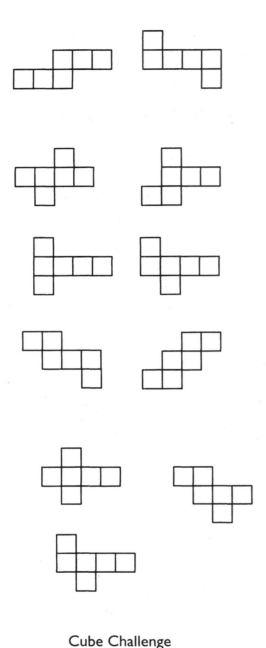

Cube Challenge

5. Cube Challenge! Ask older students to imagine how the six square faces of the cube could be arranged as a flat two-dimensional shape and then folded to create a cube. Is there only one way to form a cube? Have students work in teams to create as many cube patterns as possible. Provide grid paper to assist students with this task. To check their findings, they can cut out all the possible shapes and make cubes.

6. Create-A-Building! Give older students a duplicate of the Building Master on page 44. Have them create a building with it. In small groups, students can use their buildings to create a neighborhood. The neighborhood can include proportionally-sized driveways, cars, and people. After groups have created their neighborhoods, have the class combine their neighborhoods to create a city. Challenge students to create their own, unique building sheet patterns.

7. Origami: Have students enjoy the pleasure of folding origami figures and shapes. There are many books available on this intricate and satisfying art. *Sadako and the Thousand Paper Cranes*, a book for older students, would be ideal to read while doing an origami project.

8. Paper Airplanes: A favorite item to fold out of paper is airplanes. *The Paper Airplane Book*, a book for older students, gives new meaning to the idea of creating airplanes as it explores aerodynamics. Another book, *Wings & Things: Origami That Flies*, contains more than thirty origami models that fly, made from squares or an 8 ½" x 11" sheet of paper. Students can investigate various aspects of the airplanes they create, such as the ability to stay aloft, cover the longest distance, gain the greatest height, or display fancy "aerobatic" flight patterns.

Create-A-Shape

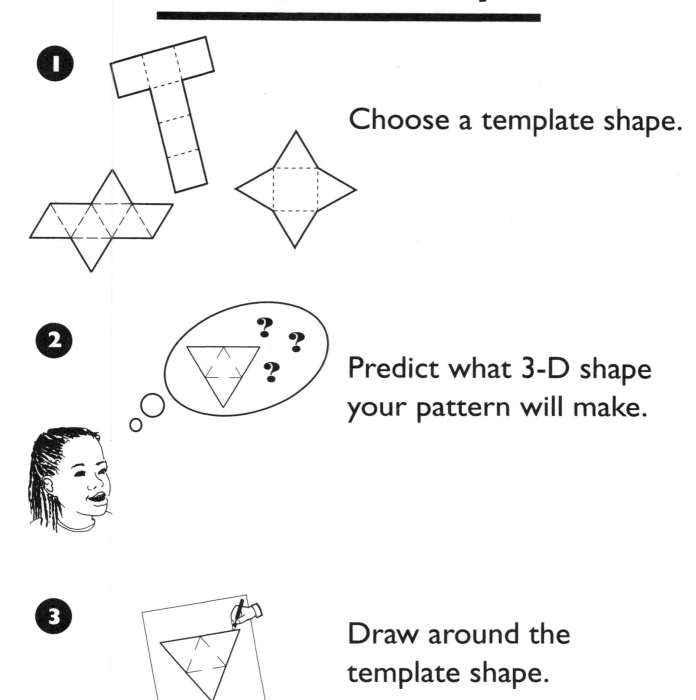

1   Choose a template shape.

2   Predict what 3-D shape your pattern will make.

3   Draw around the template shape.

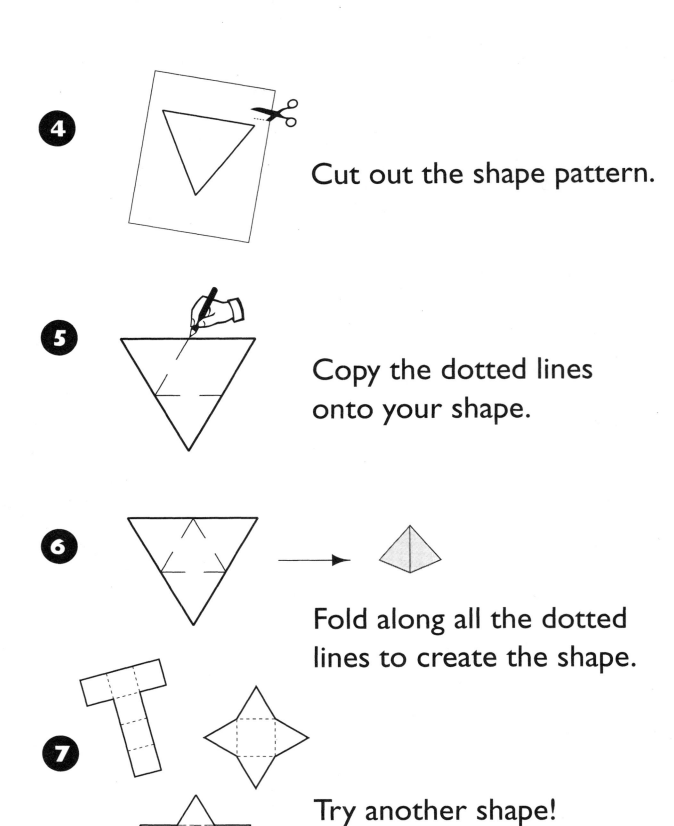

4 Cut out the shape pattern.

5 Copy the dotted lines onto your shape.

6 Fold along all the dotted lines to create the shape.

7 Try another shape!

A

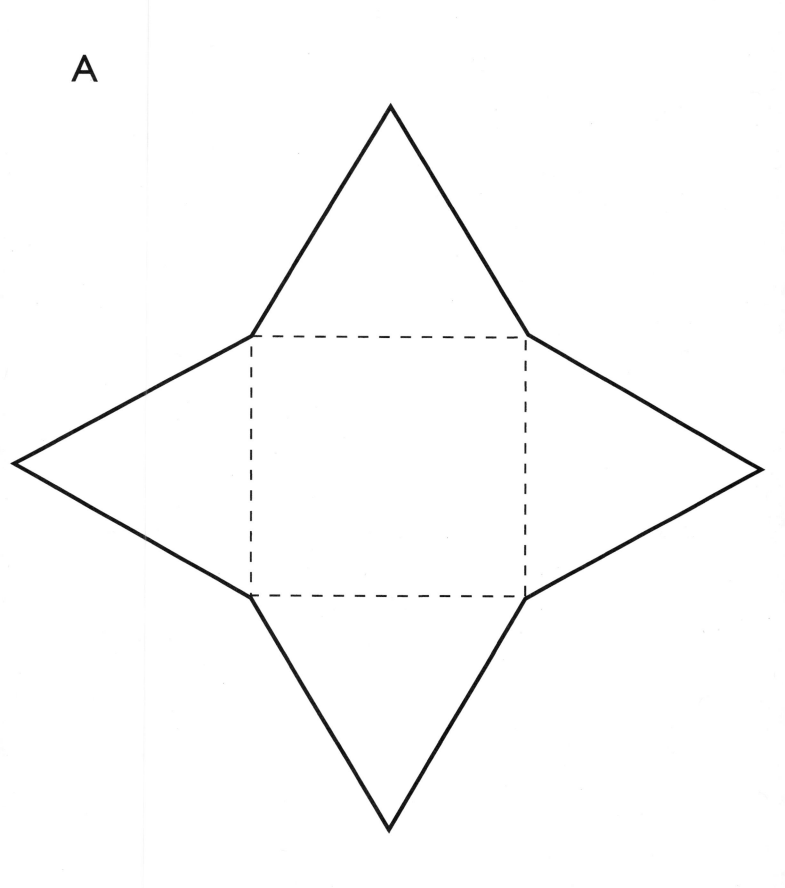

A

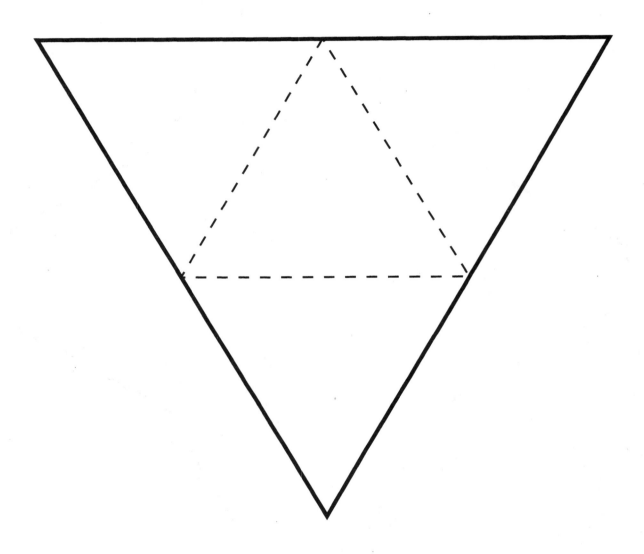

B

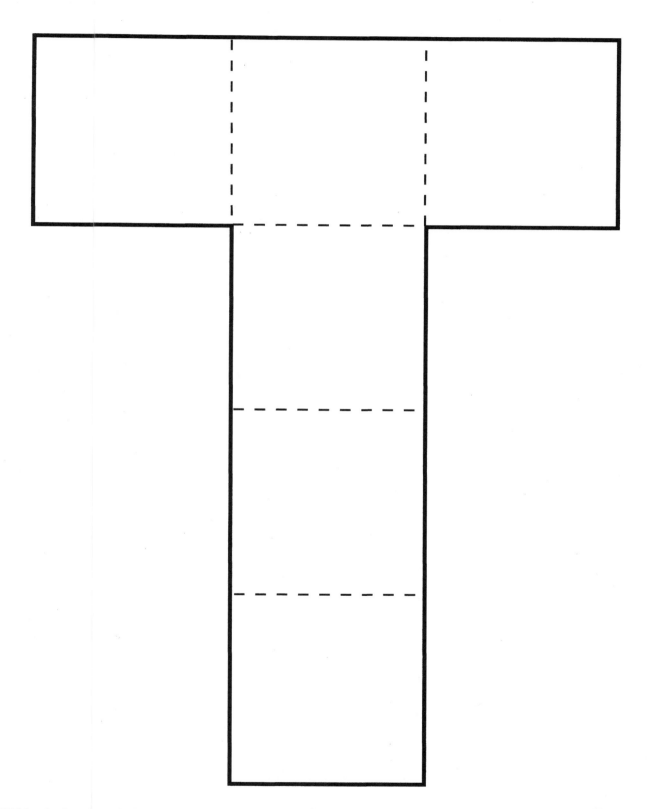

B

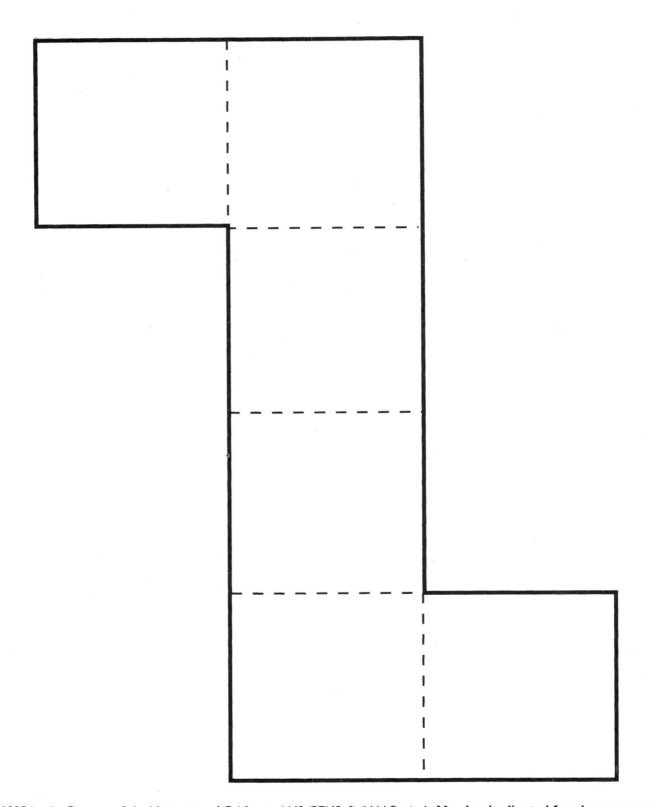

C

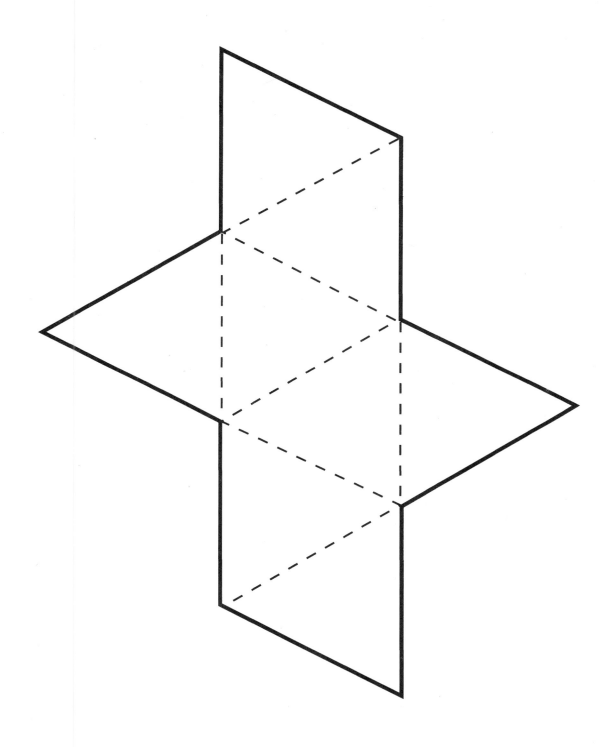

Building Master

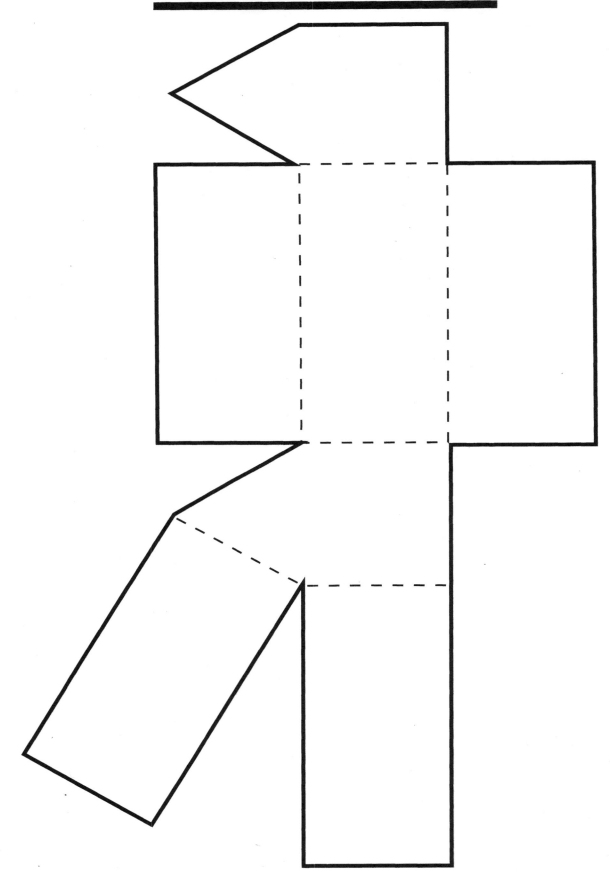

Activity 2: Dowel Designs

Overview

Architecture is a visible form of geometry that we encounter in our daily lives. Architectural structures, from the homes and buildings we see in our local communities to famous examples such as the Sears Tower in Chicago or the Empire State Building, exemplify many properties of shape, structure, and design. Other famous structures through history—including cathedrals, castles, and pyramids—also use shape in aesthetic and mathematical ways. All of these structures begin with foundations and beams that in turn create sturdy skeletons upon which to complete the structures.

In this activity, the builder in all students emerges as they create two- and three-dimensional structures out of newspaper dowels! These creations simulate the beams inside buildings. Using a recyclable material, newspaper, students roll dowels with the aid of a piece of plastic straw and tape. After several dowels are made, students use masking tape to attach dowels to dowels to create shapes and structures.

Students may initially create houses, furniture, animals, tents, bridges, kites, and free-form structures, before focusing on geometric shapes. That's fine! It is important for their creativity to flow freely! They will make many discoveries on their own. By asking questions appropriate to your students' abilities, you can assist them in making geometric discoveries about their structures. They can focus on the shapes that they used to create their structure and the number of angles and edges that it has. In addition, they are likely to discover which shape provides the most strength and stability when building larger structures!

After an initial free exploration session, students can be guided into building two- and three-dimensional structures to explore the properties of specific geometric shapes. For example, young students can count the sides and angles of two-dimensional shapes, or examine the open faces on three-dimensional ones. Older students can investigate edges, angles, and vertices on three-dimensional shapes. These models of shapes are especially good for illustrating the sides (edges), angles, and vertices of three-dimensional shapes.

Set this activity up at one or more stations and let students explore at their own pace *or* follow the steps listed on page 49 to introduce the activity to the entire class prior to having them work at the stations.

What You Need For One Station

- ❏ 20 non-flexible, plastic drinking straws, cut into thirds (60 pieces) and a few extra for your demonstration
- ❏ small container, such as a cottage cheese container, to hold the straws
- ❏ 60 sheets of newspaper in the size appropriate to your students
- ❏ 1 roll of masking tape
- ❏ 1 large sheet of butcher paper and colored markers, or an overhead projector, with transparency and transparency markers
- ❏ *(optional)* 1 Dowel Designs sign

Getting Ready

1. Decide how many stations of Dowel Designs you will need. Keep in mind that this is one of the most popular activities in this guide and all students will be eager to have a chance to build this way.

To make the straw cutting go quickly and to prevent the cut straw pieces from flying, bundle about four straws at a time into a column. Place a rubberband at both ends. Then make the two cuts necessary to divide the straws into thirds.

2. Cut the straws into thirds. To help keep the straws off the floor, put pre-cut straws in a small container at each station. Have extra pre-cut straws available.

3. Cut newspaper sheets in half—vertically down the crease. For younger students, we recommend that you cut the newspaper to one-fourth of its original size, making it more manageable for little fingers. Some teachers have even suggested cutting the paper into squares, while other have used pages from 8 ½" x 11" magazines. The shape of the paper, whether rectangular or square, matters less in this case than its overall size. All of these sizes will make acceptable dowels.

4. Set up one or more stations around the room, each with the materials listed in the "What You

Need" section. For younger students, you may want to have some 1", pre-cut pieces of masking tape ready to use to make dowels. This avoids waste of the tape and makes the process easier. When modeling how to make a dowel, emphasize using an appropriate length of tape.

5. If you are using signs, duplicate one Dowel Designs sign from pages 54 and 55 for each station.

6. *(Optional)* You may want to clear a large floor area for building a single class structure.

Special Considerations

As this activity is of such high-interest to all students, some teachers have found that it works best to do it as a whole class and over two days. On Day 1, students make their supply of dowels. On Day 2, students collaborate and build their structures. On subsequent days, students can be encouraged to further investigate geometric shapes.

The **processes** inherent in the activities at this station are more important than the product— especially for young students. Kindergarten and first grade teachers report that many of their students build flat shapes for a period of time before discovering or observing the possibility of building three-dimensional shapes. As they build two-dimensional shapes, students develop a vocabulary for these shapes, along with actual models to represent them. In addition, they may well make the important discovery that the more sides they add, the less stable the shape is!

Introducing Dowel Designs to the Entire Class

1. Demonstrate how to make a dowel:

    a. Take out a sheet of newspaper and a straw.

    b. Cut two small pieces of tape and place them in an easily accessible spot.

    c. Lay the sheet of newspaper on a flat surface.

    d. Tape the straw to one corner of the newspaper.

Several teachers suggest beginning with a pre-made building material such as Tinkertoys® or with toothpicks and marshmallows or peas. This gives the children some building experience with materials that may be easier to use than dowels and generates models for reference when building with the dowels. See the "Going Further" section on page 52.

Several teachers of older students found that it was not necessary for their students to use tape to attach the straw to the newspaper before rolling.

e. Use the straw to assist you to roll the newspaper into a dowel.

f. Tape the dowel closed so it will retain its shape.

2. Have two students model how to make a dowel cooperatively. After they have completed a dowel, use theirs and the one you made to model how to attach the two dowels to one another using tape.

3. Depending on the skills and abilities of your class, you can have students work independently, with a partner, or in small groups to make dowels. With the dowels, they can make a shape or structure—flat (two-dimensional) or three-dimensional. It is probably a good idea to have them make at least six dowels before starting to build something. If working in groups, be sure to have students discuss their ideas for a structure before starting to attach dowels together.

4. Circulate around the class assisting as necessary. Pose questions such as:
- What things in the classroom (real world) are similar to your shape/structure?
- What geometric shapes are in your structure?

a. In the case of two-dimensional shapes, ask more specific questions, including:
- How many sides does your shape have?
- Do any other shapes have that number of sides?
- How many angles does the shape have?

b. If students have built three-dimensional shapes, ask:
- How many edges does your structure have?
- How many angles does your structure have?
- How many vertices does your structure have?

Note: Although some students may be able to visualize the faces on the shapes, it may also be helpful to have students use newspaper to actually make faces and put these on their structures so they can clearly see the faces created by the dowels.

Sharing Shapes and Structures

1. Have students share their shapes and structures with the class. After this festive activity, you can help summarize the experience in many ways. Here are some options:

- Connect their structures to real world examples.

- Sort the two-dimensional and three-dimensional shapes. Review the geometric names and attributes for the flat shapes.

- Explore the stability of shapes. Which structures are the most stable? What shapes were used to create them? Are the tall structures stable?

- Identify the structures that are polyhedra. (See "Behind the Scenes" on page 193.) Make a chart to record each shape with a picture and its name. Have students identify and count the number of faces (vertices or edges) on each shape. Sort these shapes by the number of faces (vertices or edges). Compare and contrast the shapes with the same number of faces (vertices or edges).

You may want to record on the chalkboard, a large sheet of butcher paper, or an overhead transparency for a permanent record.

2. On a subsequent day, you may want to have students work with a partner to build specific three-dimensional shapes, such as a tetrahedra.

a. Use dowels to pre-make a model of a tetrahedron.

1.) Hold up your model. Ask students how many dowels are needed to construct it. [6]

2.) Ask, "What shape are all the faces?" [Triangles]

3.) Count the angles and/or vertices, if appropriate, for your students.

b. Have pairs of students make the six dowels.

1.) Ask how many dowels are needed to construct one triangle. [3] Have students build that triangle.

2.) Challenge students to complete the tetrahedron using yours as a model. Walk around and offer assistance as needed.

c. Review attributes of the shape, such as number of edges, angles, faces, and vertices.

d. (*Optional*) Some teachers have had their students connect all of the individual tetrahedrons to make one large tetrahedron.

e. Have students build other polyhedra. As each new one is made, compare it to the previous ones.

Going Further

1. **Structures to Inhabit**: Have students design tents and homes for stuffed animals. Can they build a large enough structure to fit in themselves? Completed structures can be painted with tempera paint.

2. **Peas and Toothpicks**: Provide peas (previously soaked dry whole peas) and toothpicks, or marshmallows and toothpicks, to create small models of three-dimensional shapes, as well as free-form structures. Challenge older students to attach paper faces to their structures.

3. **Tinkertoy® Structures**: Use giant or small Tinkertoys to build three-dimensional structures. Construct-o Straws® are another commercially produced building material similar to dowels.

4. **Builders at Work**: Visit a construction site so the students can observe the skeleton of a building before the walls go up. What shapes do they notice?

5. **Ancient Architecture**: David Macaulay has done a series of detailed, architectural books on ancient structures, including a medieval castle, an Egyptian pyramid, a Welsh castle, and a Roman city. These authentic books examine how shapes are chosen to serve many functions. They can provide inspiration for students as they build their structures. See listings in the "Literature Connections" section of this guide.

6. **Fly A Kite!** Use dowels, bamboo, or straws to create the structure for a kite. Then cover it with tissue paper and try it out! Students can experiment with their designs to find kites that fly the highest. *Kite Craft* (listed in the "Resource Books" section) is a good reference book on the history and processes of kitemaking throughout the world.

7. **Shape Descriptions**: Have younger students use newspaper dowels (or peas and toothpicks) to build a two-dimensional figure, such as a triangle, square, pentagon, etc. Then ask students to describe the characteristics of the figures. Share descriptions to define the characteristics of shape. Make a book with the definitions and illustrations of the shapes. Older students can follow the same procedure for three-dimensional shapes, such as a pyramid, a tetrahedron, and a cube.

Dowel Designs

1 Tape a piece of straw down on one corner of a piece of newspaper.

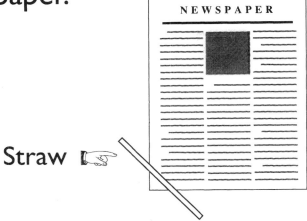

Straw ☞

2 Use the straw to help you roll up your newspaper into a dowel.

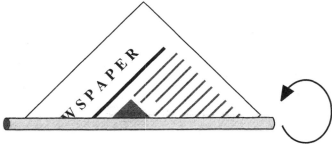

3 Tape your dowel closed.

4 Make more dowels.

5 To connect your dowels together—lay the ends of your dowels across each other, fold the ends over and tape them together.

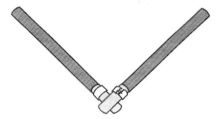

6 Make additional dowels and create 3-D shapes!

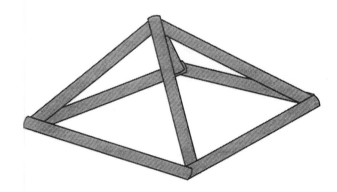

Dowel Designs Challenges

Can you make a pyramid?

Can you make a tetrahedron?

Can you make the tallest structure?

Can you make a structure using only triangles?

Can you make a bridge?

Activity 3: Polyhedra

Overview

In this activity, students enthusiastically construct three-dimensional creations with high-interest building materials: snap-together triangles, squares, and pentagons. The figures that the students make serve as *models* of polyhedra. Polyhedra are three-dimensional, closed figures that are formed by polygonal surfaces. Each of these polygonal surfaces is called a "face." (See the Geometric Glossary in the "Behind the Scenes" section on page 193 for more information.)

The intriguing and inviting material in this activity lends itself to open-ended exploration and creativity—students can construct houses, geodesic domes, and even spinning tops. After building their own polyhedra, students create specific three-dimensional geometric figures and develop the mathematical vocabulary for them with a focus on the faces. Students can make a variety of polyhedra with the same number of faces. Then students make comparisons between these different three-dimensional figures—such as the difference between a cube and a rectangular prism.

Set this activity up at one or more stations and let students explore at their own pace *or* follow the steps listed on page 61 to introduce the activity to the entire class prior to having them work at the stations.

What You Need For One Station

- ❏ 50 snap-together triangles
- ❏ 50 snap-together squares
- ❏ 25 snap-together pentagons
- ❏ (*optional*) Polyhedra signs

An open-ended challenge sheet is included on page 65.

See the "Sources for Materials" section on page 213 for sources for these materials. Be sure to have an adequate number of building pieces at each learning station. The 125 pieces recommended here should work well for up to six students.

Getting Ready

1. Decide how many learning stations of Polyhedra you intend to set up.

2. At each station, place a variety of plastic shapes on a flat surface for building.

3. If you are using signs, duplicate one or both of the Polyhedra signs from pages 66–69 for each station.

4. Right before introducing the activity, gather several triangles, squares, and pentagons to model how to connect the material.

5. Make a cube using four squares of one color for the sides of the cube and two squares of a different color for the bases. This cube will be used by students later in the activity after they have had a chance to freely build.

Special Considerations

Students love this activity and usually need lots of time to build their own creations before following specific directions. As they build, they discover the possibilities and limitations of building with these three shapes. They may even build shapes whose names they do not know! On the other hand, some young students may build flat shapes before considering the possibility of three-dimensional shapes. Allow them the time they need for that as well as to gain dexterity in connecting the pieces.

This is a fabulous activity, but it is expensive because of the cost of the building material! You may want to purchase one set of materials for a single station for your class. Alternately, your school could purchase a large class set that can be shared by your entire school.

Although these shapes look very sturdy, they can be broken! Occasionally, the "teeth" (connecting parts) break off, rendering the piece useless for building. Be sure to discuss "polyhedra care" beforehand.

One teacher felt that this activity was a "natural, hands-on way to teach geometric properties."

Introducing Polyhedra to the Entire Class

1. Hold up the triangle and have students identify it. How many sides does it have? [3] Ask if they know any other type of triangle. You may want to have students come to the board to draw other types of triangles. (See page 196 of "Behind the Scenes" for information on triangles.)

2. Next hold up the square. Have the students identify it and count the number of sides. [4] Is there any other way to make a square? Why or why not?

3. Finally, hold up the pentagon. Count the number of sides. [5] Ask what the name of this shape is. If students suggest other names for the pentagon, use this opportunity to draw the shapes that they suggest. Count the number of sides on these other polygons. (See page 197 of "Behind the Scenes" for more information on polygons.)

4. After you have identified each of the three shapes, tell the students that these three shapes are all polygons. A polygon is a two-dimensional shape with three or more sides. Ask what polygons they see in the classroom. Include rectangles, hexagons, trapezoids, etc. Students may suggest circles. Discuss whether or not circles are polygons. Do they have sides?

5. Tell students that they will use these polygons to build three-dimensional shapes. Hold up an example of a three-dimensional object in the classroom. Compare it to one of the two-dimensional polygons.

6. Model how to snap the shapes together. You do not need to build a three-dimensional structure for the students. Invite them to use the polygons to create three-dimensional shapes and structures. Mention (as noted earlier) that the shapes are breakable—especially the connecting parts—so they should be careful as they build.

7. Have students go to learning stations and allow them enough time to freely explore the shapes and create their own three-dimensional figures.

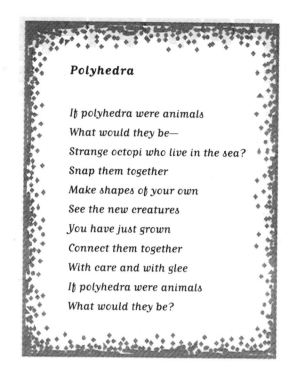

Polyhedra

If polyhedra were animals
What would they be—
Strange octopi who live in the sea?
Snap them together
Make shapes of your own
See the new creatures
You have just grown
Connect them together
With care and with glee
If polyhedra were animals
What would they be?

An overhead projector also works well to model how to snap the shapes together.

Discussing Shapes, Exploring Faces

1. After the students have built a variety of figures, have them come to an area away from the tables with the building materials. Alternately, students can stay at their places and put their completed pieces in the center of the table. It is challenging for many students to listen to a discussion while still at a table with this high-interest material.

2. Hold up a cube. Ask what things in the real world are this shape. Ask for the name of this shape. If appropriate for your students, introduce the geometric term for this shape—hexahedron.

3. Ask what shapes were used to make the cube. [squares] How many were used? [6] Be sure to count them! Tell the students that on three-dimensional shapes the flat surfaces are called "faces." In the case of the cube, all the faces are the same shape—squares.

Building three-dimensional models of polyhedra with the three polygons lends itself to an exploration of the faces of polyhedra.

4. Ask a student to bring a closed shape other than a cube to the discussion area. Have students predict how many faces it has. Count the faces. What are the shapes of the faces?

5. Have students return to their tables to examine the faces on the shapes that they have created. Have them sort all the closed three-dimensional shapes by the number of faces.

6. Continue the exploration of faces by having students build as many different shapes as they can with six (or any number) faces. After a building period, have students examine the shapes they have made. Check that they all have six faces. Compare and contrast the shapes.

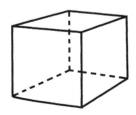

7. Depending upon your students' experiences and abilities, subsequent activities with these shapes can include an exploration of edges and vertices.

Going Further

1. **Comparing Pyramids**: Have students make a pyramid with a square base and four triangular faces. Then have them make a tetrahedron—a pyramid made up entirely of triangles. Use a triangle for a base and attach three other triangles to form the faces. Compare and contrast these two shapes.

2. **Making a List, Checking it Twice**: Develop a class list of characteristics of polyhedra. This enables students to compare and contrast the characteristics (number of faces, edges, angles, and vertices) of different geometric figures. Older students can keep a journal of their findings.

3. **Polyhedra Plans**: Have students write up directions for building geometric figures. Then, they can challenge others to build using their instructions!

4. **Octahedron Exploration**: Challenge students to build a polyhedron with eight faces. What shapes do they need to build it? Can it be made more than one way?

5. **Platonic Solids**: Investigate the five Platonic solids which include hexahedrons, tetrahedrons, octahedrons, dodecahedrons, and icosahedrons. What shape is used to build each one? How many shapes are needed? Have students do research about these shapes and present reports on them to the class.

6. **Euler's Formula**: The Swiss mathematician Leonhard Euler (pronounced "Oiler") discovered that the number of faces, vertices, and edges of a regular polyhedron are related according to the following formula:

Number of Faces + Number of Vertices =
Number of Edges + 2
        or
$$F + V = E + 2$$

Older students can discover the same relationship that Euler did by being asked to explore the relation between the number of edges (E), faces (F), and vertices (V) of polyhedra. This activity is best done in the context of an investigation where student are **not** given the formula at the outset. Have students build models of the polyhedra and then construct a "T-table" to record the number of faces, vertices, and edges as shown below. Then encourage students to find and articulate some relationships between the number of faces, vertices, and edges.

Polyhedra	# of Faces (F)	# of Vertices (V)	# of Edges (E)
Cube 	6	8	12
Tetrahedron	4	4	6
Octahedron	8	6	12
Dodecahedron	12	20	30
Icosahedron	20	12	30

Open-ended Challenge

To create your own polyhedron, use any of the flat squares, triangles, and pentagons to build your own 3-D shape.

Polyhedra

To Make a **Pyramid**:

1 Take 1 square and 4 triangles.

2 Start by placing the square flat on the table.

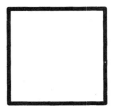

3 Attach a triangle to each side of the square.

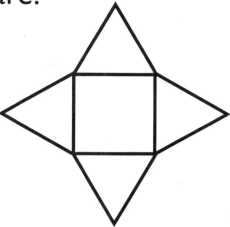

4 Fold up all the triangles until they meet at a common point and connect them.

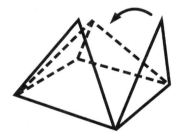

5 You have made a pyramid!

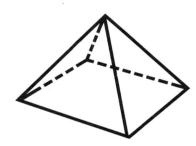

Polyhedra

To Make a **Tetrahedron**:

1 Take 4 triangles.

2 Start by placing one triangle flat on the table.

3 Attach the other three triangles to the sides of the first triangle.

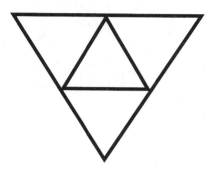

4 Fold up all the triangles until they meet at a common point and connect them.

5 You have made a tetrahedron! It is also a pyramid!

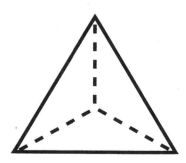

Activity 4: Fill-A-Shape

Overview

In this activity, students have fun as they fill shapes in a variety of ways with colorful pattern blocks. Using small wooden pattern blocks, students fill star, triangle, hexagon, and dodecagon shapes that are outlined on pieces of card stock. As students fill the same shape more than one way, they discover relationships among the pattern block shapes.

For example, the star shape can be filled with one hexagon and six triangles or it can be filled with two trapezoids and six triangles. In this case, the discovery is that the hexagon can be made with two trapezoids! The star can be filled many other ways as well, thereby giving students an opportunity to see and experience more than one solution to a single problem!

This activity reinforces the names and properties of geometric shapes and their relationship to one another. Students develop spatial sense as they fill the large shape forms with pattern blocks. In addition, as students discover different ways to fill in the same shape, they explore congruence and equivalence. Older students can go farther and investigate area.

Set this activity up at one or more stations and let students explore at their own pace *or* follow the steps listed on page 73 to introduce the activity to the entire class prior to having them work at the stations.

*As students fill the shape cards, the are working in the area of mathematics known as **discrete mathematics**. As the word "discrete" implies, this math strand involves separate, countable quantities and also includes the ways that those quantities can be arranged. For example, in this Fill-A-Shape activity, students fill each shape card with a finite, countable number of pattern blocks. The combination of pattern blocks used to fill a particular shape is one discrete solution. Using those very same pattern blocks, other unique solutions can also be determined by changing the arrangement of the pattern blocks. These multiple solutions are the permutations of this combination of blocks. This aspect of discrete mathematics falls under the heading of combinatorics. For more information on discrete mathematics, see the "Building Hexagons" activity on pages 76 and 77 in the "Going Further" section.*

What You Need For One Station

❒ 1 set of pattern blocks
❒ 6–12 shape cards
❒ *(optional)* white or colored card stock
❒ *(optional)* 1 Fill-A-Shape sign

Getting Ready

1. Decide how many Fill-A-Shape learning stations you want to set up.

2. Decide in advance whether you will have all students begin with the same shape to fill at each station, or if there will be a variety of shapes from which students can choose. (Having all students begin with the same shape to fill is highly recommended for younger students.)

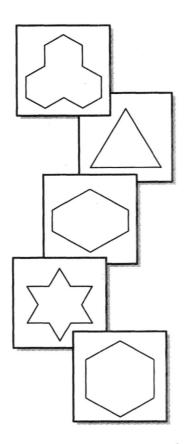

    a. If all students will fill the same shape, duplicate enough copies of that shape (see the Hexagon Shape Masters sheet on page 80) on card stock, so that each student at the station has one copy of the shape to fill with pattern blocks.

    b. If the students will have a choice of shapes to fill, duplicate enough copies of each shape (see the Shape Masters sheet on page 81) on card stock, so that each station has a few copies of each shape.

Note: When duplicating the shape master sheets, it is helpful to use different colors of card stock for the different shapes.

3. If you are using signs, duplicate one Fill-A-Shape sign from pages 78 and 79 for each station.

4. Set up one or more stations around the room with materials listed in the "What You Need" section.

5. Gather a small number of pattern blocks and one shape to fill for your demonstration.

Special Considerations

This activity works best when students have had an opportunity to freely explore the pattern blocks before being asked to fill a shape.

For younger students, it is best to choose one shape that all the children will fill at the same time. This will provide an opportunity to look at multiple solutions to the same problem.

The pattern block squares and tan parallelograms do **NOT** work in any of these large shapes! This is an important discovery for the children to make for themselves. (However, squares and parallelograms will work in a regular dodecagon.)

For older students, you may want to add the regular dodecagon shape. Its twelve equal sides and angles allow for more challenging ways to Fill-A-Shape. Because all the pattern blocks can be used, the number of possible combinations increases dramatically, as does the sophistication of the design work! In addition, your students can use the dodecagon shape to do the other Fill-A-Shape activities. In this revised edition of the guide, you will find the "Dodecagon Shape Masters" sheet on page 204.

Introducing Fill-A-Shape to the Entire Class

1. Gather students in an area away from the stations to model how to fill a shape. First hold up the shape you want to fill. Have students identify the shape.

2. Fill the shape with pattern blocks so that no pattern block goes outside of the perimeter (edges of the shape) and so that there are no spaces inside the shape not covered by pattern blocks.

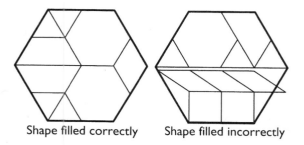

Shape filled correctly   Shape filled incorrectly

You could also model how to fill a shape on the overhead projector, using overhead pattern blocks.

3. Ask students if they think there are other ways of filling that same shape. Explain that they will be filling shapes in a similar fashion. Students can work individually or with a partner.

    a. Have **younger students** use the same shape you used in your demonstration. Send them to stations with that shape and have them try to fill the shape in as many ways as possible. After they build the shape one time, have them slide the pattern block shapes off the paper carefully so that they keep the form of the shape that they built, and build again. Can they use all the different pattern block shapes to fill the shape?

b. Give **older students** a choice of shapes to fill. Hold up the various shapes for them to identify. Challenge them to fill the same shape more than one way. Have students record the various ways that they filled the shape. Can they use all the different pattern block shapes to fill the shape?

4. Circulate around the room as the students are filling shapes. Offer assistance as necessary and ask questions to encourage investigation, such as, "Can you fill that shape another way?" or "Can you use just seven pieces to fill that shape?" or "Can you use all the different pattern block shapes to fill the shape?" Ask if they can fill the **same shape** with the **same pattern blocks**, in a **different way**. If students are filling a variety of shapes at a learning station, ask if they can fill a **different shape** with the **same pattern block** pieces they used for the shape they just completed.

Fill-A-Shape

Fill a shape and fill it well

Just like words that letters spell

Shapes within others

Help everyone see

The beauty of geometry!

Going Further

1. **Shape Recipes!** Develop a recipe file for each of the shapes. After students have filled a shape with the pattern blocks, they can record the "recipe" for others to create. Be sure students list the ingredients first! Young students can record pictorially and older students can embellish their recipes with directions on how to make the shape. Using the star shape, young students could record their recipe by just writing or drawing the ingredients as follows:

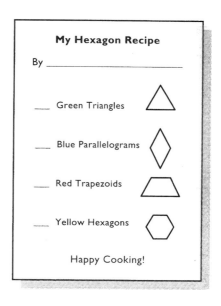

Older students may write a recipe as follows:

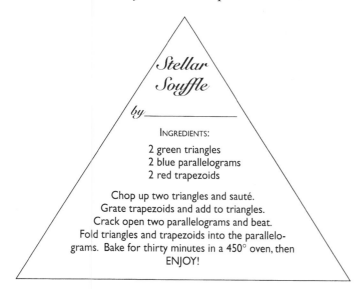

Slip in some recipe cards with recipes that do NOT work! Have students alter them so they do.

2. **"Cookin' with Pattern Blocks" Cookbook:** One teacher reported that her class published a cookbook after completing the recipe activity. Each student contributed one recipe complete with the ingredients

and the "shape" that was being "prepared." In the back of the book, they placed an envelope with a copy of each of the shapes and many paper pattern block shapes. Students read the book and cooked the shapes. The book was a big hit when they took it home to share with their families.

3. **Make My Shape!** Choose one shape to investigate as a group. Have students fill that shape. Have one student propose a way to fill that shape by telling the pattern blocks she used to fill it. Have all students attempt to make the shape with pattern blocks. Did everyone create a shape that looked the same? How many solutions were there? Do more solutions exist?

4. **Challenge Me!** Choose one shape to explore. Have students fill the shape with the fewest number of pattern blocks possible. Now, can they fill it with exactly eight pattern blocks? Try filling the box with only trapezoids. Fill it with thirteen blocks. Predict the largest number of pattern blocks needed to fill the shape. Ask students to explain how they arrived at their prediction.

5. **New and Unusual Shapes**: Have students select six to twelve pattern blocks. Create a flat shape with no inside spaces using those pattern blocks. Trace around the outline of the shape. Have students fill each others' shapes.

6. **Shape Books**: *The Secret Birthday Message* is a delightful story book for young students that uses shapes in an inviting format. Young students will be inspired to create their own shape books. See "Literature Connections" on page 207 for other book suggestions.

7. **Building Hexagons:** Older students can explore how many ways there are to build a hexagon that is the same size as the yellow pattern block hexagon, but using the other pattern block shapes. Ask students to predict how many ways they think they can build the hexagon, then have them proceed. There are different answers, depending on the way students interpret the problem of "how many ways." If the **order of placement** of the different pattern block shapes is **not** taken into account, then there are eight different ways to build the hexagon. In this case, students are exploring all the various possible *combinations* of pattern blocks to make the hexagon. However, if students include as a variable the order of placement

of each pattern block piece as they build each of the eight hexagons, then they are exploring all possible *permutations*! This is a very challenging task. Depending upon the abilities of your students, you may want to define the task more specifically at the onset, or start with the combinations and then move to the permutations. This problem falls under the heading of "discrete mathematics." Discrete math has to do with counting principles—the emphasis being on separate, countable quantities. There is a finite, countable number of combinations for any given set of objects. In this case, by using a systematic method of organizing the pattern blocks, your students will be able to determine the finite number of both combinations and permutations. Each is discrete and the total number can be counted. Discrete mathematics also intersects with probability and statistics. Take, for example, the toss of two dice. There is a countable number of outcomes that can be represented by both combinations and permutations. The analysis of the discrete data generated by the tosses will determine what toss is theoretically most probable. The GEMS guides *Frog Math, Group Solutions II, In All Probability, Math Around the World*, and *QUADICE* all contain additional activities and useful background information that explore these and related mathematical concepts.

Combinations of Pattern Blocks to Build a Hexagon

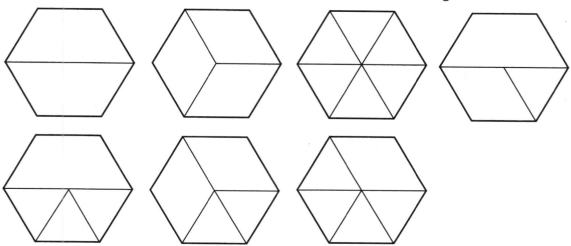

Permutations of one combination: the trapezoid, parallelogram, triangle

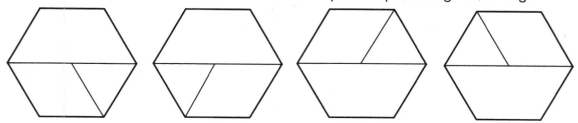

Additional rotational permutations of this combination
developmentally appropriate for high school and college students

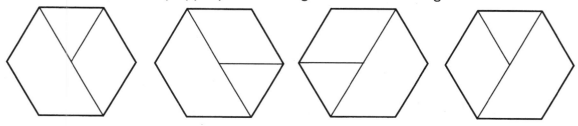

Fill-A-Shape

1 Take a shape card.

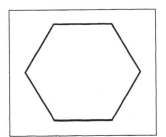

2 Fill the shape with pattern blocks so that the shape is completely filled. Be sure no pattern blocks go outside the shape.

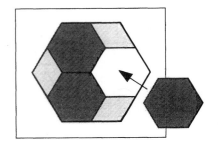

3 Slide your pattern blocks off the shape.

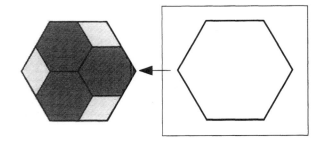

4 Fill the same shape
again in a different way.

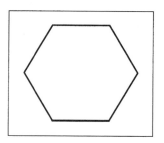

5 How many different
ways can you fill the
shape?

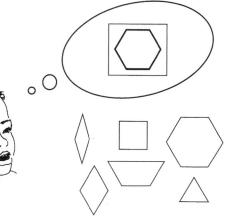

6 Can you use all of the
different pattern block
shapes to fill in the
shape?

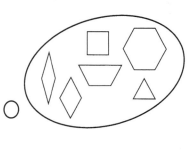

Hexagon Shape Masters

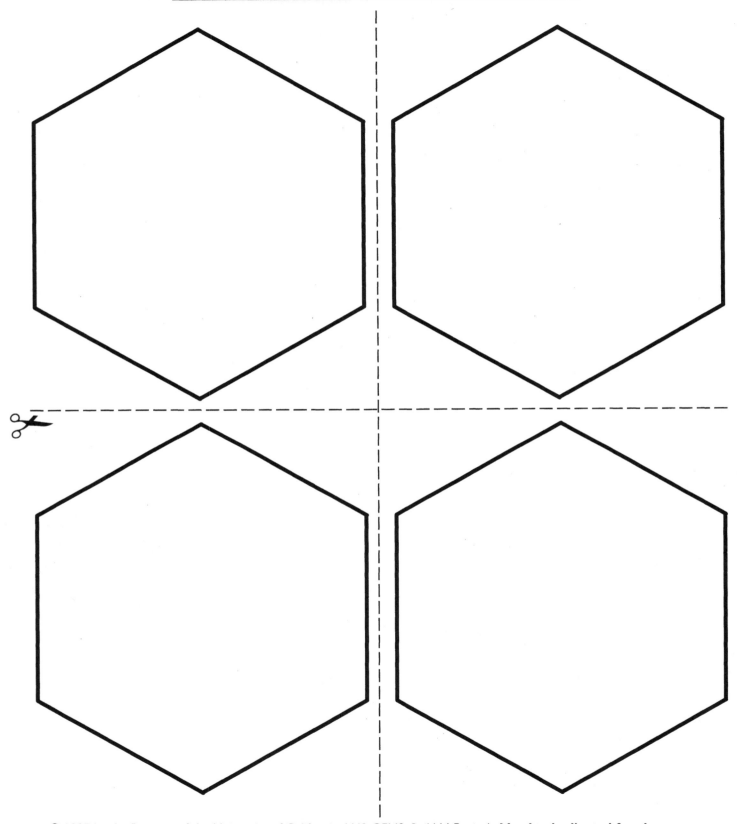

Shape Masters

Activity 5: Symmetry

Overview

Look at the wings on a butterfly, the spots on a ladybug, a plant leaf, or the shell of a scallop. These are but a few examples of things from the natural world that have bilateral symmetry.

In this activity, students explore bilateral symmetry as they make designs with pattern blocks. Using a card that has one-half of a design, students first fill in that half with pattern blocks. Then they complete the other half of the design symmetrically, using additional pattern blocks. Students also have opportunities to create their own beautiful bilaterally symmetric designs with pattern blocks.

Set this activity up at one or more stations and let students explore at their own pace *or* follow the steps listed on page 85 to introduce the activity to the entire class prior to having them work at the stations.

Bilateral symmetry is illustrated when folding a symmetrical object (such as a sheet of paper) in half. The fold line is the line of symmetry and it divides the object into two halves so that the resulting two parts on either side of the line match exactly. Not all objects have a line of symmetry while other objects may have more than one line.

What You Need For One Station

- ❏ 4–8 symmetry cards
- ❏ 1 set of pattern blocks (250 in a standard set)
- ❏ (optional) white card stock
- ❏ (optional) 1 Symmetry sign
- ❏ (optional) several mirrors

Getting Ready

1. Decide how many stations you intend to set up.

2. If your students have not had much experience with the concept of bilateral symmetry, consider first teaching the Body Symmetry activity (described in the "Special Considerations" section) and/or the art activities (described in "Going Further") as pre-activities.

3. Select the symmetry designs from the Symmetry Masters on pages 90–120 that are appropriate for your students. Those marked with an "A" are the most basic. Duplicate your selection(s) on white card stock and if possible laminate or cover with clear contact paper. (You may also want to create symmetry design cards of your own.)

4. If you are using signs, duplicate one Symmetry sign from pages 88 and 89 for each station.

5. Set out the materials listed in the "What You Need" section.

6. If you are introducing the activity to the entire class, select a symmetrical design to use to model the activity for your students, and gather enough pattern blocks to build it.

Special Considerations

Students without much prior experience with symmetry often just copy the pattern block design instead of creating the symmetrical half. If your students have had few opportunities to explore bilateral symmetry, do pre-activities on symmetry as described above. This will give students an understanding of bilateral symmetry **before** they work with the pattern blocks.

Introducing the Symmetry Activity
to the Entire Class

1. Ask students what they know about symmetry. Hold up a symmetrical design card. Point out that half of the design is on the card. Explain that they will first use pattern blocks to fill that in, then they will build a matching design on the other side of the line.

2. Model how to build the design.

   a. First, place the appropriate pattern blocks on the half of the design that has the pattern block shapes outlined. Leave them there.

   b. Count the number of each of the pattern blocks you used. To create the other half of the design, take that many additional pattern blocks of each shape.

   c. Working from the line of symmetry, complete the other half of the design with the pattern blocks.

3. Have students go to stations and work in pairs or independently.

4. As you circulate, be sure that students are actually building the other half of each symmetrical design and not solely placing blocks on the printed side or only making an exact, but non-symmetrical, copy of the given side on the other. Assist students as necessary. If a card seems too easy for a student, challenge that student to add more pattern blocks to the first side of the design, and then build the symmetrical half.

Some teachers have chosen to first build a symmetrical design with giant size pattern blocks. The students can help place pattern block shapes on the design.

Optional: Use a mirror to check. Place the mirror on the line of symmetry so that it will reflect the pattern blocks on the second half of the design. Does it match the first side? (Note: Simple mylar mirrors work well. See page 216 for one source.)

Pre-Activity: Body Symmetry

1. Recruit a student volunteer to stand up in front of the class.

2. Tell the students that, to help them imagine a line drawn down the middle of the child from head to toes, you are going to use a piece of yarn (the line of symmetry). Place the yarn vertically on the student so that it divides the student in half.

*Children may notice things that are **not the same** about **both** sides of the child, such as a bracelet or ring on one hand and not the other, or even a hole in one pant knee and not the other. Older students may discuss more detailed differences between, for example, two ears or eyes, or may also mention internal body organs, such as the heart or stomach, which are not mirrored on the two sides of the body, i.e., not symmetrical. Acknowledge these accurate observations! Point out that the human body has some things which are symmetrical and some things which are not. For your information as the teacher, it is worth noting that while many, but not all, of the main external physical features of humans do have a basic symmetry, it is certainly not exact, and many of the internal structures of the human body are not symmetrical. The object of this part of the activity is to provide young children with a basic sense of what symmetry means and the ways in which their own bodies reflect this concept.*

You may want to look for things in the room that are symmetrical. See also the Scavenger Hunt suggestion in the "Going Further" section.

3. Point out that there is an eye on each side of the yarn. Ask the students what other things are the **same on *each* side** of the yarn. [Ears, nostrils, eyebrows, hands, arms, toes, legs, knees, shins, etc.]

4. Now put the yarn across the volunteer's waist. Look at both sides of the yarn. Ask if the volunteer is the same on both sides of the yarn. What is opposite of the head? [Feet!] What is opposite of the arms? [Legs!] Are they the same? [No!] Doing this can help children see that the body has only one line of symmetry.

Going Further

1. **Symmetry Art Activities**: Students both young and old can gain an insight into symmetry through the following art activities:

Squish Paintings: Paint a picture on one half of a piece of paper, fold the paper in half and press down. Open and look at the two symmetrical sides. For a more dramatic effect, children may want to cut around their design and paste it on a colored sheet of paper.

Cutouts: Fold a sheet of paper in half. Beginning at the fold, cut out a free-form shape from the paper. Open up the shape—both sides are the same! Have students decorate the sides symmetrically with crayons, felt pens, or pencils. Suggest cutting simple shapes, such as butterflies, hearts, and ovals, as well as making additional cuts on either side of the shapes.

Hole Punches: Have students fold a sheet of paper in half. Punch several holes in the folded sheet. Open up and observe where the holes are. Students can decorate around the holes symmetrically.

2. **Scavenger Hunt**: Have students discover other symmetrical objects or designs in the classroom, school, or at home. Some teachers suggest that their students' weekly "sharing" object be something symmetrical. Students can "prove" the symmetry of the object by using a piece of yarn as the line of symmetry. Keep a record of these findings in a class journal.

3. **Museum of Symmetry!** Students can develop a classroom display or "museum" of symmetric designs and objects. Have them show the line(s) of symmetry on each object.

4. **Shape Symmetry**: Have students find lines of symmetry for geometric shapes such as a square, equilateral triangle, isosceles triangle, oval, trapezoid, pentagon, hexagon, circle, etc. For younger students, model with a large rectangular sheet of paper. Ask children to predict how many ways there are to fold the rectangle so that two identical halves are created. Take a suggestion and fold the paper. If it works, use a crayon to draw over the line of symmetry. Continue until all lines are drawn. Before they begin with a shape, have partners predict how many lines there will be. After two shapes are done, have students compare the lines of symmetry between them. Continue comparing the lines of symmetry as the exploration continues.

5. **Grid Designs**: Have students fold a sheet of 100-square grid paper in half. Color in one half of the design. Then complete the other half symmetrically. Challenge older students to fold the paper twice so that there are two lines of symmetry. Then they can color in the grid symmetrically.

6. **Symmetrical Masks**: One teacher reported that students had fun cutting out a shape for a mask from a folded sheet of paper. Then students decorated their mask symmetrically. They also investigated masks from other cultures and examined them for symmetry and asymmetry.

7. **Pattern Block Quilt**: Have students look at quilt designs in books or at home. Are all designs symmetrical? Do some quilt designs have more than one line of symmetry? Give each student a 6" square sheet of white paper. Have them build their own unique symmetrical design on it with pattern blocks. Record the design on a 6" sheet of black paper with paper pattern block shapes. (See the "Sources for Materials" section for where to purchase paper pattern block shapes.) Create a class quilt by gluing each of the squares onto a large, colored sheet of butcher paper. See the "Literature Connections" section for stories to accompany this activity.

Symmetry

(apologies to William Blake)

Kitty, kitty, leaping light

Through the grassy forest bright

Eyes and ears and whiskery

Such a cheerful symmetry!

Symmetry

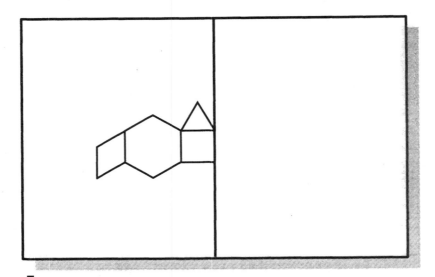

1. Choose a card.

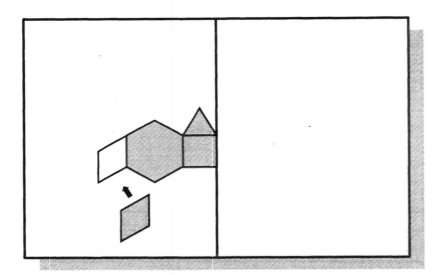

2. Cover the design with pattern blocks.

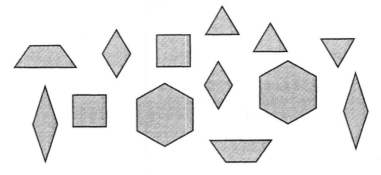

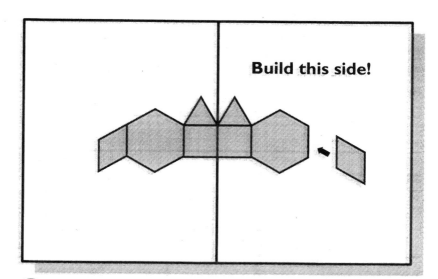

Build this side!

3. Now build the other half of the symmetrical design. *You will need to use the same pattern blocks that you used for the first half.*

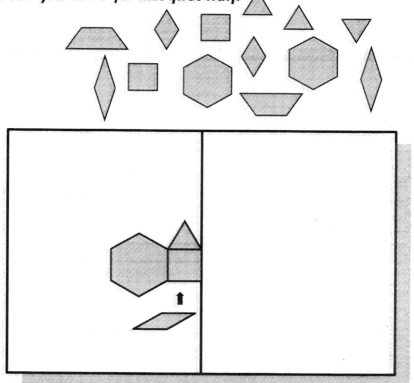

4. Now create your own symmetrical design.

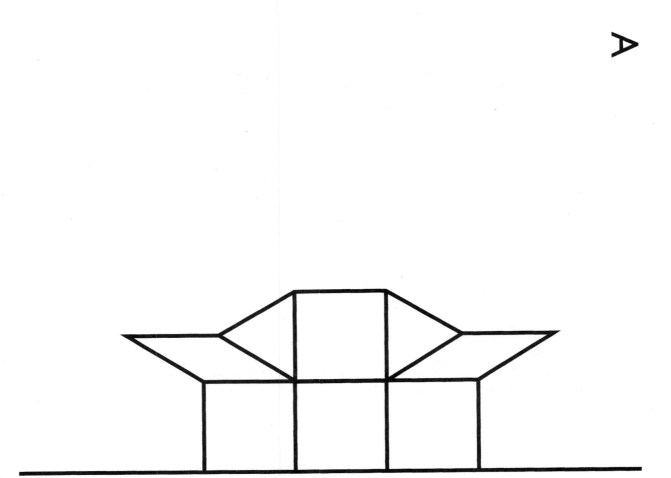

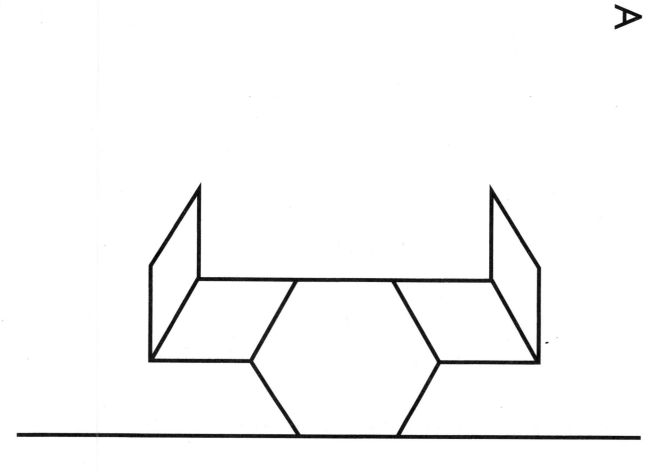

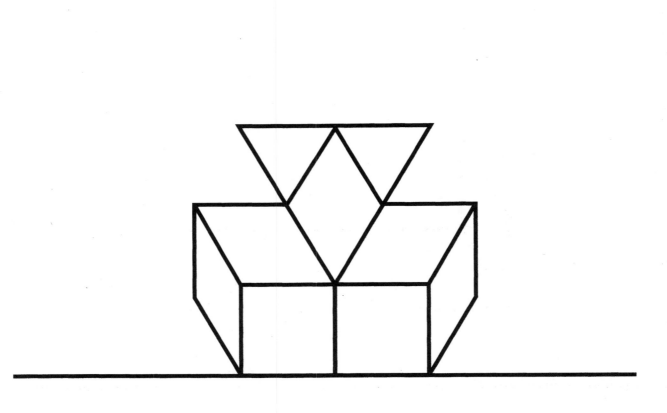

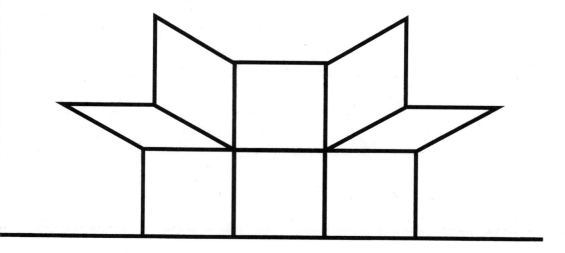

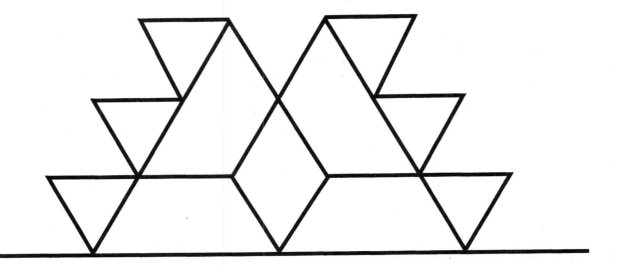

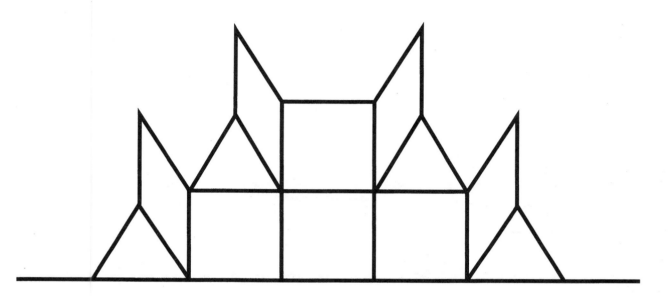

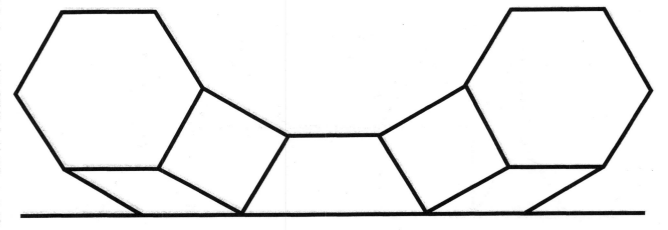

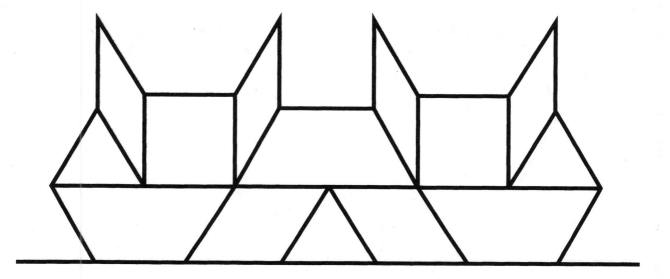

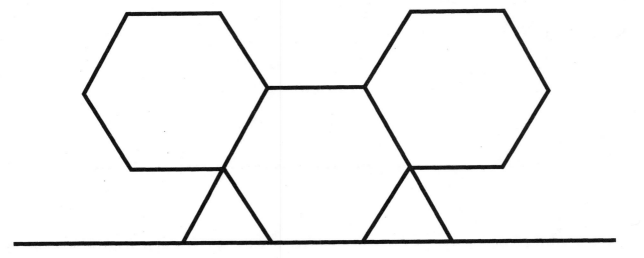

A

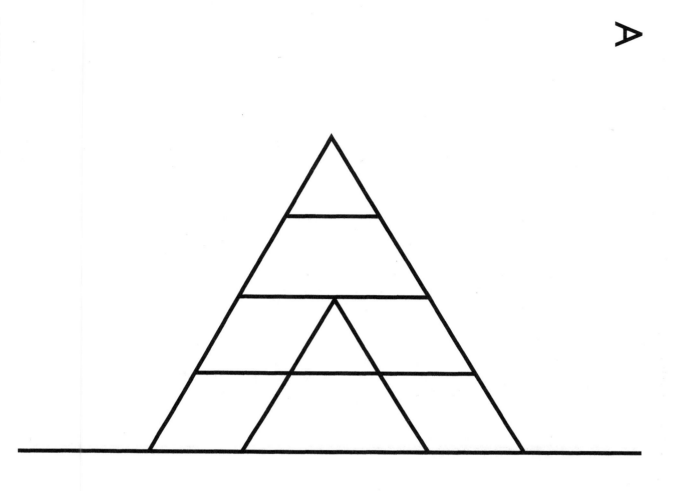

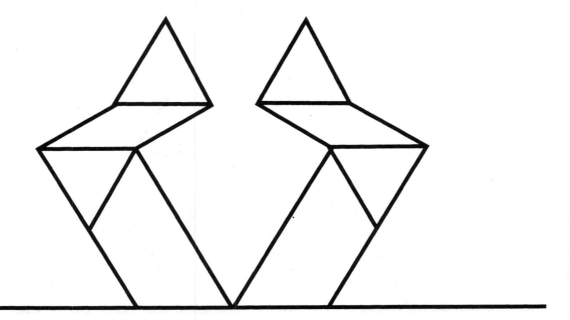

B

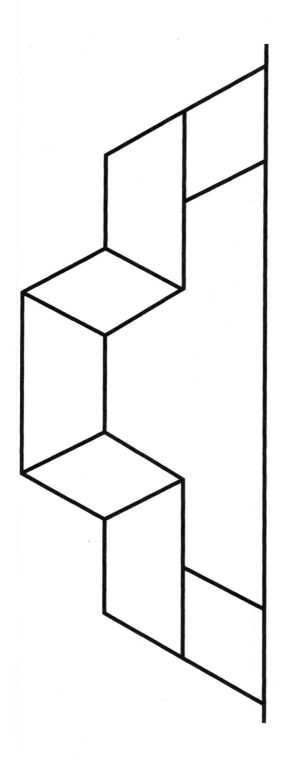

B

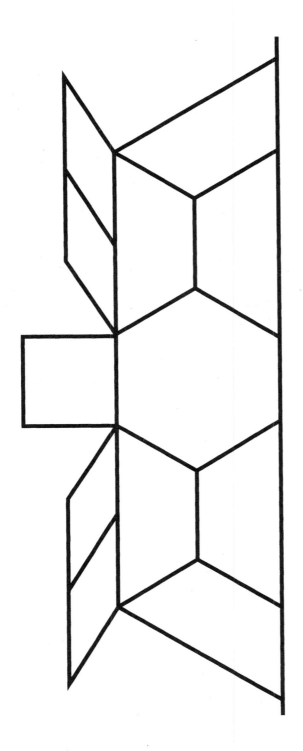

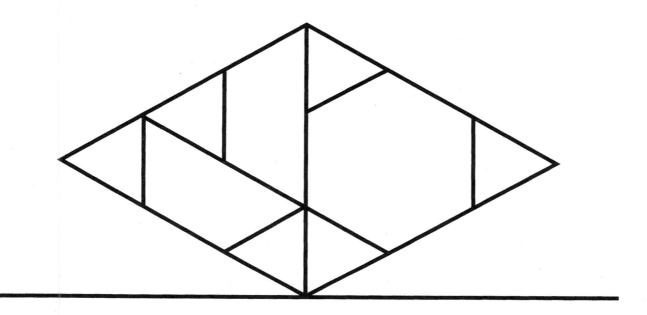

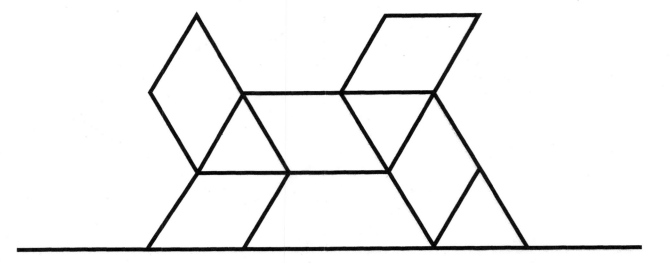

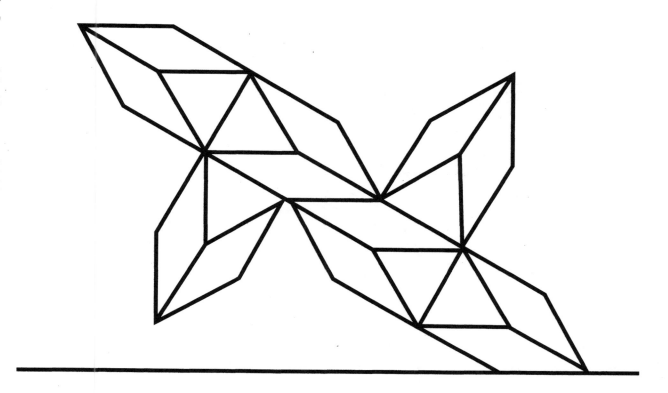

B

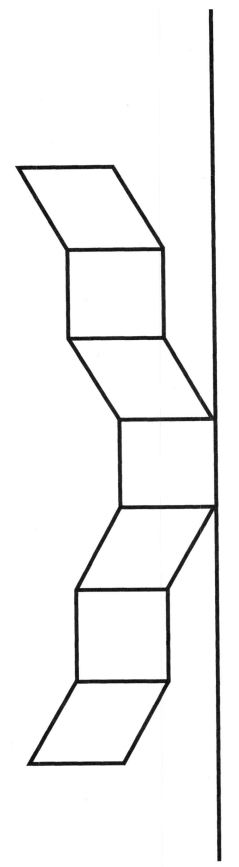

B

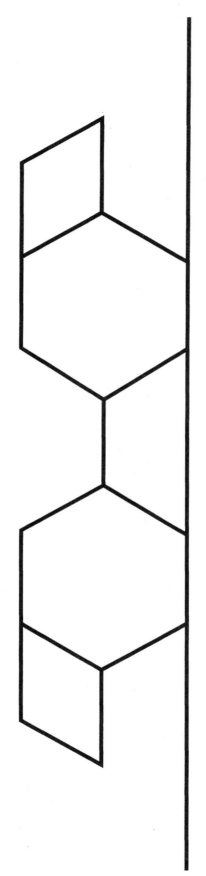

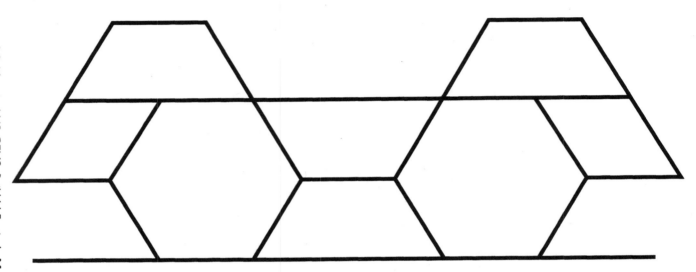

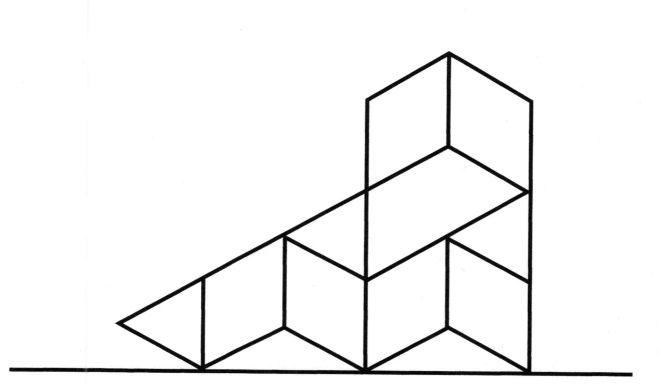

B

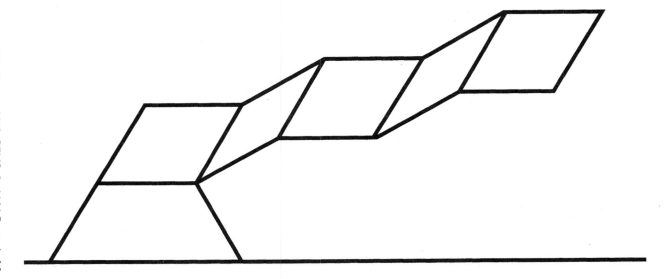

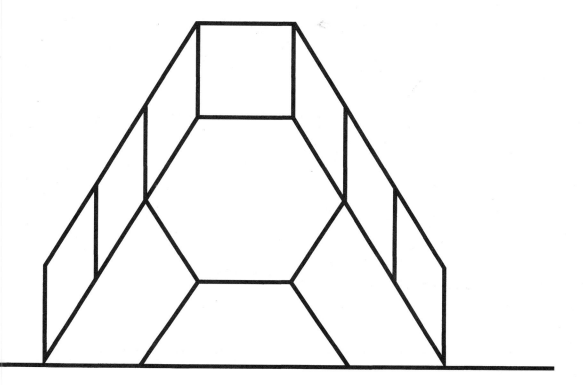

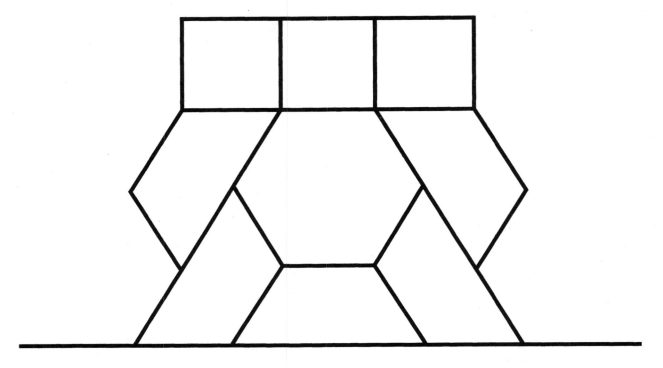

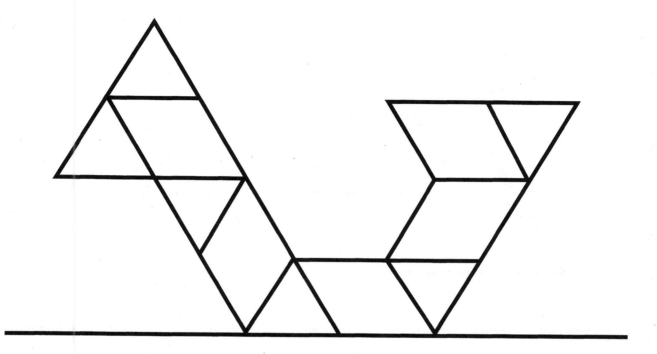

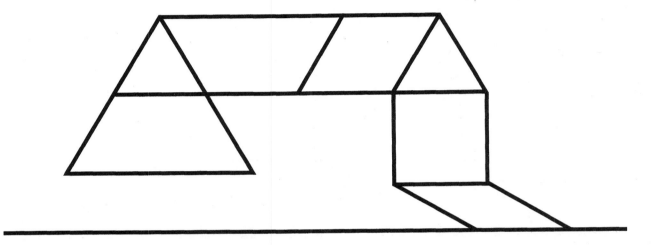

B

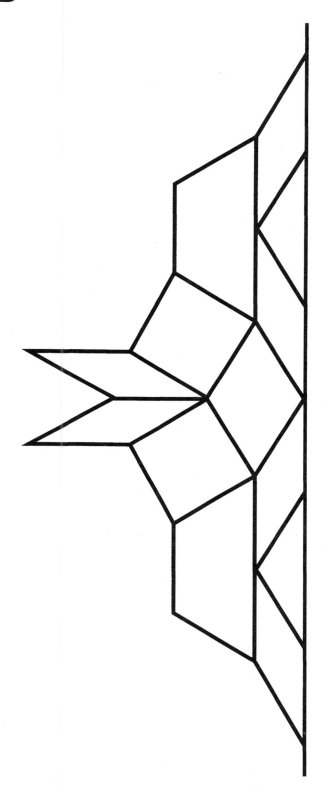

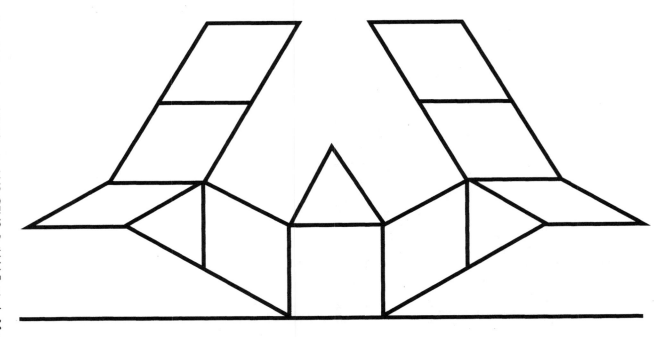

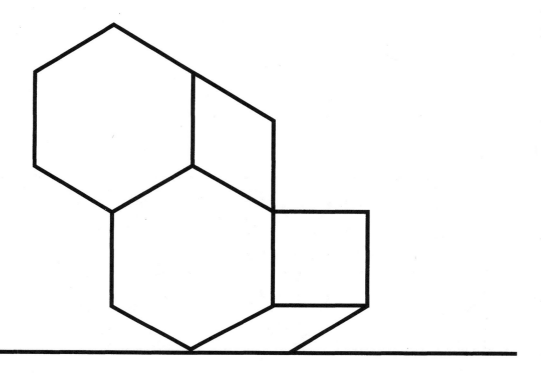

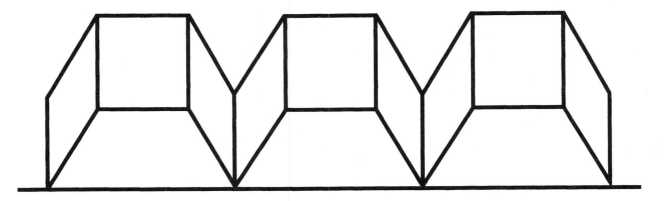

B

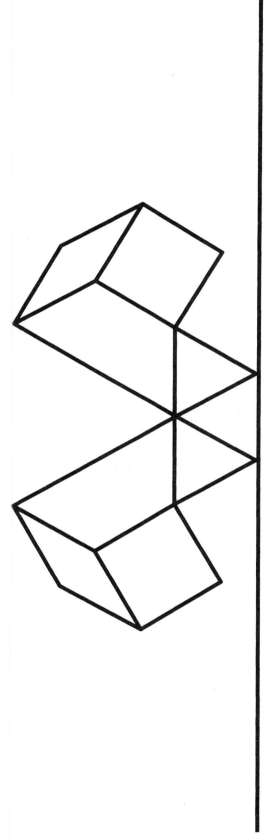

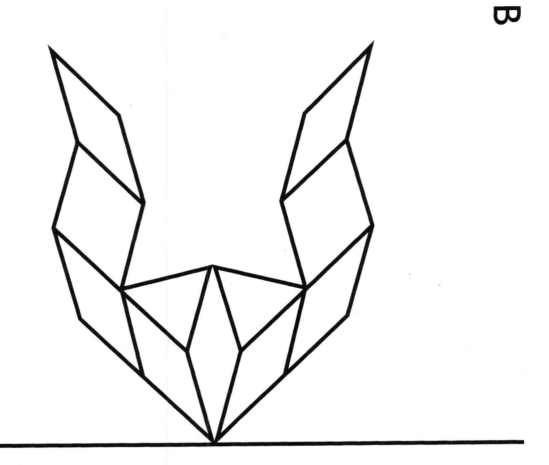

Activity 6: What Comes Next?

Overview

In this activity, students figure out or "decode" patterns constructed out of pattern blocks and then continue building the pattern. The patterns vary from simple ones, such as an "ABAB" pattern (green triangle, orange square, green triangle, orange square, etc.) to more advanced patterns, such as the pattern of squares (one square, two-by-two square, three-by-three square, etc.). At each station, there can be a variety of patterns. After building pre-made patterns, students can have fun creating their own!

Pattern is a major underlying theme in all of mathematics. A pattern can be found in anything that repeats itself over and over. Looking for patterns helps develop logical thinking and the ability to solve problems and predict future events. As the mind searches for patterns, sense can be made from what at first may appear to be discrete, separate, and unrelated things or events. There are many patterns found in nature and life cycles—looking for and finding patterns of growth and change is one of the most powerful analytical tools in science and mathematics as well as in human knowledge and perception.

Set this activity up at one or more stations and let students explore at their own pace *or* follow the steps listed on page 124 to introduce the activity to the entire class prior to having them work at the stations.

What You Need For One Station

- ❏ 1 set of pattern blocks (250 in a standard set)
- ❏ 6 pre-made pattern cards
- ❏ (*optional*) white card stock
- ❏ (*optional*) What Comes Next? signs

> ### What Comes Next?
>
> Devise a pattern
> Help it grow
> Doing this
> Will help us know
> Patterns spring up
> Everywhere
> On the land and in the air
> Some hard to see
> But don't be vexed
> Just work at finding
> What comes next!

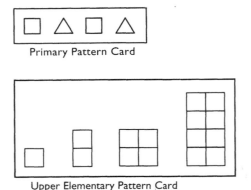

You may also want to create your own pattern cards at the level of your students. See page 126 for some suggested patterns to create for students to decode and then continue to build. Use paper pattern block shapes to build the first three or four elements of the pattern on a card.

Primary Pattern Card

Upper Elementary Pattern Card

The book Mathematics Their Way *is a valuable resource for more activities on pattern. See the Pattern Block Wall activity in the "Going Further" section.*

Getting Ready

1. Decide how many What Comes Next? stations you intend to set up.

2. Duplicate the appropriate pattern cards from masters on pages 133–140 on white card stock. Simplest patterns are labeled with an "A." You may want to laminate these cards for greater durability.

3. If you are using signs, duplicate one or both of the What Comes Next? signs from pages 131 and 132 for each station.

4. For younger students, have sets of pattern blocks ready to distribute during the first session. Set up station(s) during subsequent sessions.

5. For older students, set out the pattern blocks, pattern cards, and a sign at each station.

6. If you will be introducing the activity to an entire class of older students, then draw the first elements of a pattern on the chalkboard so that the pattern will repeat itself one time. Tape individual sheets of paper (or use large post-its) over each element of the pattern, so you can later reveal them one at a time.

Introducing What Comes Next? to the Entire Class

With all students, begin by asking them what they know about **patterns**. Encourage them to give real world examples. Look for patterns on clothing such as the stripes on someone's shirt, or create a pattern with a line of students using a repeating characteristic to make the line such as long hair/ short hair or wearing jeans/not wearing jeans, etc.

For Younger Students

1. You may want to introduce pattern with a rhythmic pattern, such as a repeating "clap, snap, clap, snap....." pattern.

2. When students are familiar with the pattern, model how to translate the rhythmic pattern into a concrete pattern using two pattern blocks, such as the green

triangle and orange square. Build the pattern as long as the length of your arm.

3. Then have students say the pattern several ways, such as by color (green, orange, green, orange...), shape (triangle, square, triangle, square...), and with the words (clap, snap, clap...) to connect the rhythmic pattern to the actual materials (pattern blocks). Point out that the pattern remains the same, even though it can be expressed many different ways.

4. Next, introduce another simple rhythmic pattern, such as a "clap, clap, snap..." pattern. When the children know the pattern, have them go to stations to build the pattern with pattern blocks. Let them know that they can choose *any two* pattern block shapes to build the pattern. Have them build the pattern at least as long as their arms.

5. Circulate and have children say their patterns to each other. Encourage them to build the same pattern another way or make a new pattern.

6. On subsequent days, set up stations with pre-made patterns. Increase the level of challenge as students are ready.

For Older Students

1. Focus the attention of your students on the board. Tell them that there is a pattern hidden behind the sheets of paper. Their challenge is to decode it.

2. Remove the first sheet. Have students note what is behind the sheet. Remove the next sheet. Ask if anyone can predict the next element in the pattern.

3. Continue to ask for their predictions and remove the sheets one by one until all sheets are removed. Be sure all students know the pattern.

4. Let students know that they will decode patterns at the stations. Hold up a sample of the pattern cards. Explain that the first few elements of each pattern are already built and their challenge is to continue building the pattern.

5. Have students work individually or with a partner.

6. Circulate and ask focusing questions such as: "Can you build the tenth element of the pattern without building all the elements in between?"

Some teachers have put a pattern on the overhead projector for students to continue. Other teachers have drawn the first elements on the chalkboard for students to copy and then continue to build on.

Some teachers have their students record their patterns by drawing the shapes or colors of the shapes, or by gluing paper pattern block shapes, on long, thin strips of paper.

Paper/post-its covering the rest of pattern

Suggested Patterns to use in Introducing What Comes Next?

1. **Sequential** (simplest to more complex):

   a. ABABAB...

   □ △ □ △

   b. AABAAB...

   □ □ △ □ □ △

   c. ABBABB...

   □ △ △ □ △ △

   d. ABCBABCB...

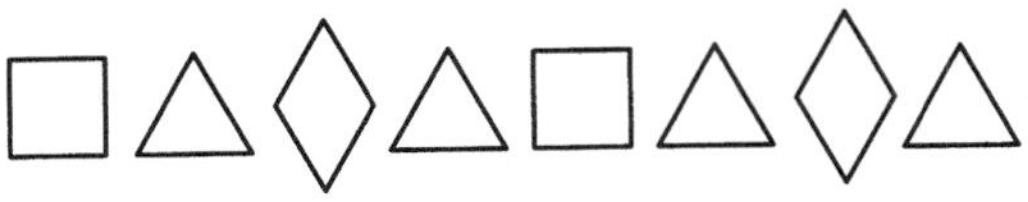

   □ △ ◇ △ □ △ ◇ △

   e. ABBCABBC...

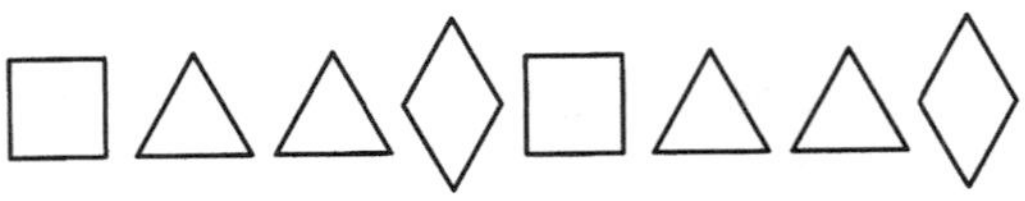

   □ △ △ ◇ □ △ △ ◇

   f. AABCCAABCC...

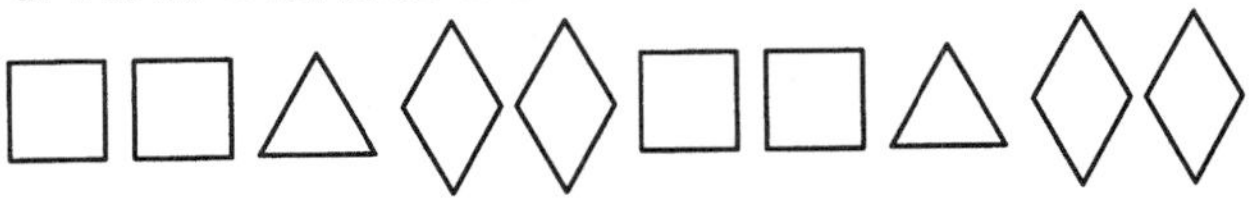

   □ □ △ ◇ ◇ □ □ △ ◇ ◇

   g. ABABCABABC...

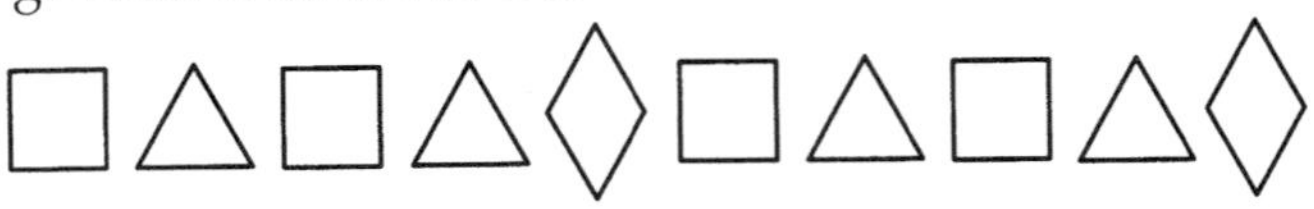

   □ △ □ △ ◇ □ △ □ △ ◇

   Other more advanced patterns, such
   as ABCACABCAC..., can be built. Be
   sure the pattern repeats itself at least
   TWO times.

2. **Numeric** (use the same shape pattern block to build each element of the pattern):

    a. **Addition:** +1 pattern (or plus any number) can be done several ways including these two:

      1.)

      2.)

    b. **Doubling (multiplication):**
x 2 pattern (or times any number)

      1   2   4   8

3. **Geometric** Generations or squares of the same pattern block shape (1, 4, 9, 16, ...):

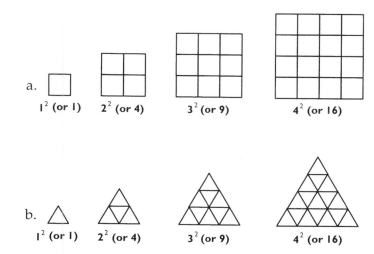

a. 1^2 (or 1) 2^2 (or 4) 3^2 (or 9) 4^2 (or 16)

Challenge your students to build generations or squares with the other pattern block shapes. Is it possible with all shapes? (All except the hexagon.)

b. 1^2 (or 1) 2^2 (or 4) 3^2 (or 9) 4^2 (or 16)

4. Open-Ended Pattern: First two elements only! By giving only the first two elements of a pattern, the problem becomes much more open-ended and students have to explain their thinking! For example, build the beginning of the geometric square pattern. With the square pattern block, build only the first two elements of a square pattern—with 1 block and 4 blocks. Ask what comes next and for an explanation of why that comes next! Possible answers can include: nine (square pattern); seven (plus three added to each step); or 16 squares resulting from doubling the sides of the first square. See what your students suggest!

Pattern for students:

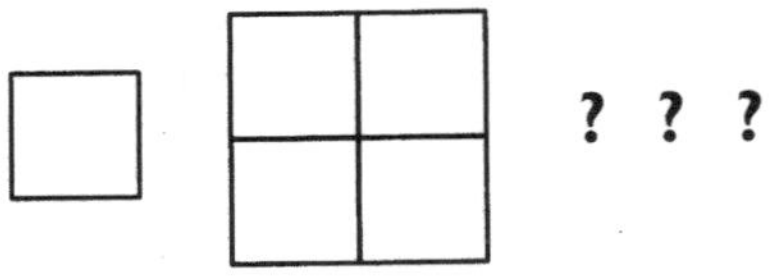

? ? ?

Possible next elements:

1.)

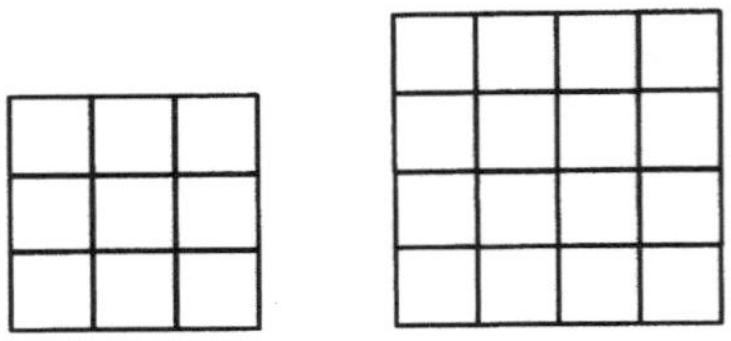

(etc. if interpreted as a square pattern)

2.)

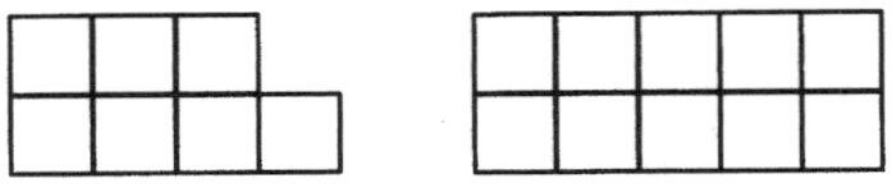

(etc. if interpreted as a "+3" pattern)

3.)

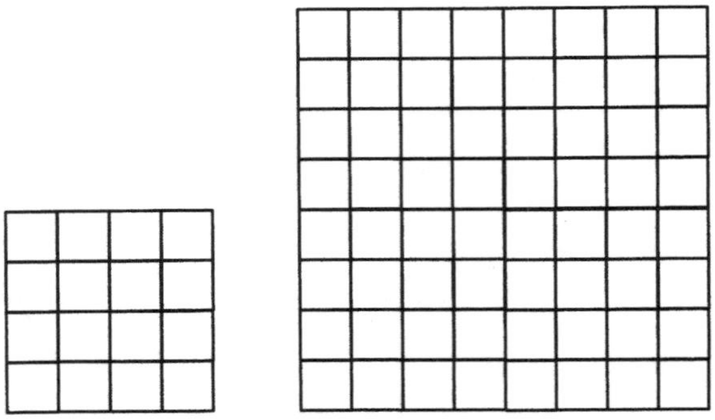

(etc. if interpreted as a doubling the side of square pattern)

5. Advanced Pattern: Fibonacci's Number (1, 1, 2, 3, 5, 8, 13, 21, 34, 55, 89,...) each number being the sum of the previous two numbers. Build the first SIX elements of this pattern! Ask your students, "what comes next?"

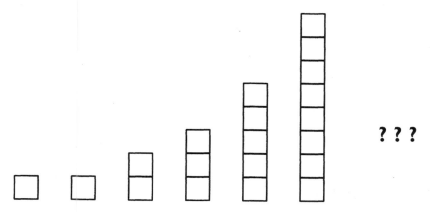

Note: Many examples of this pattern exist in nature. For example, in a pine cone, eight rows can spiral gradually or 13 parallel rows can spiral steeply. Other examples include artichokes, pineapples, and sunflowers.

Going Further

1. **Pattern Block Walls**: This is an excellent pattern activity from *Mathematics Their Way*. In this activity, students use pattern blocks to build pattern block walls. See the "Resource Books" section for where to obtain this excellent resource.

2. **Build and Build Again!** Introduce a pattern appropriate to your students' ability level with rhythmic movements. When students are familiar with the pattern, have them choose a manipulative and build it so that the pattern repeats at least ten times (or as long as the length of an arm). Record the pattern with pictures, colors, rubber stamps, or symbols across the length of a sheet of paper. Then take the recorded pattern and choose another manipulative to build the pattern again! Record the pattern a different way.

3. **Pattern Necklaces**: Younger students can make pattern necklaces using breakfast cereals such as Fruit Loops™, dyed macaroni, or small pieces of colored plastic straws.

4. **Pattern Story Books**: Read stories that feature repeated verse, such as *Brown Bear, Brown Bear, What Do You See?*, then as a class create a pattern book to accompany the story. Another book, *The Snowy Day*, has clear examples of repeating pattern as a young boy creates patterns with his feet and a stick. Students can use crayons, paint, or markers to create artistic patterns. See "Literature Connections" section on page 207 for other books related to pattern.

5. **Geometric Pattern Books**: *A Grain of Rice* and *The King's Chessboard* are two books that illustrate the pattern of exponential growth. In each story, a single grain of rice is doubled every day and the reader sees how quickly the amount of rice grows with this pattern.

6. **Calendar Patterns**: At the end of a month, have students look for appropriate number patterns in the calendar. For example, young students can circle the pattern of 2 or of 5 on the calendar, while older students might see if they can find numerical patterns in the diagonal lines.

7. **Calendar Literature**: For young students, there are many delightful books that connect with the pattern of the days of the week as well as months of the year. *Chicken Soup With Rice* is a humorous look at the months of the year.

What Comes Next?

1. Look for a pattern.

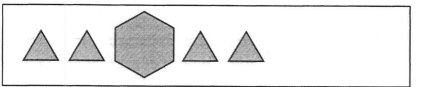

2. Continue the pattern!

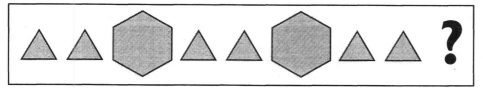

3. How far can you extend the pattern?

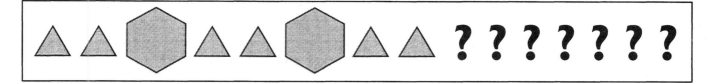

4. Build a pattern of your own.
Challenge your partner to continue it!

What Comes Next?

1. Look for a pattern.

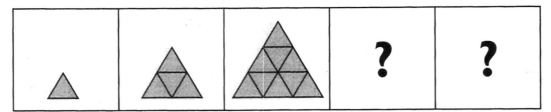

2. Now build the next two steps of the pattern.

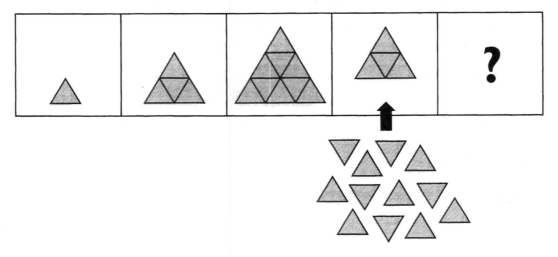

3. How far can you extend the pattern?

4. Can you build the 10th element of the pattern?

5. Build a pattern of your own.
Challenge your partner to continue it!

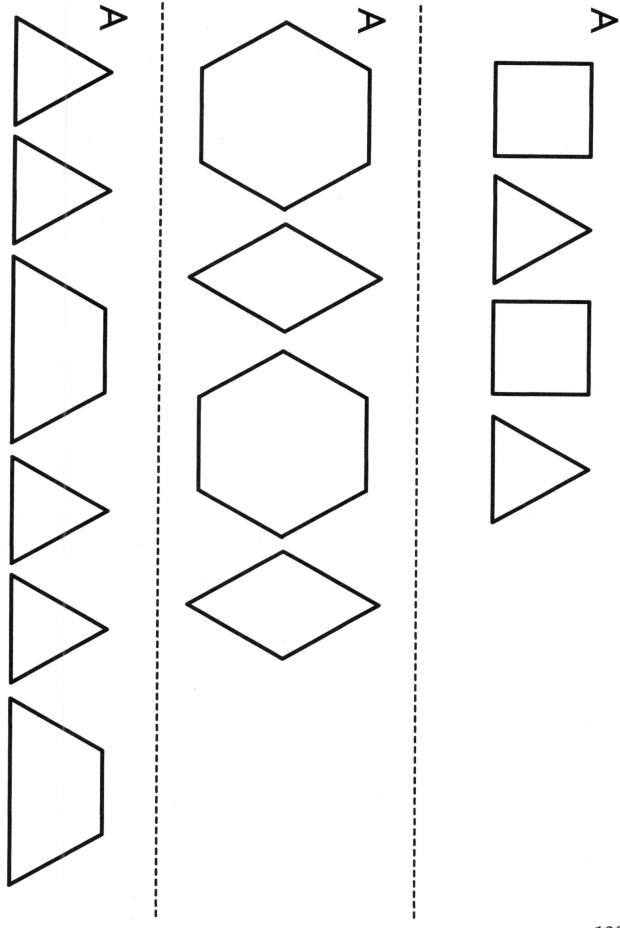

A

A

A

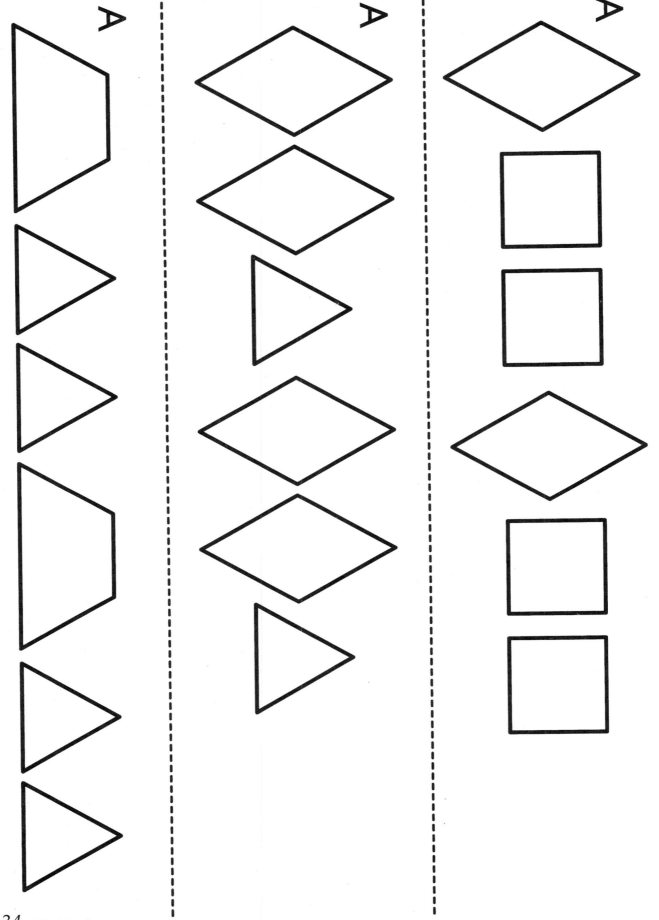

A

A

A

B

B

B

B

B

B

B

C

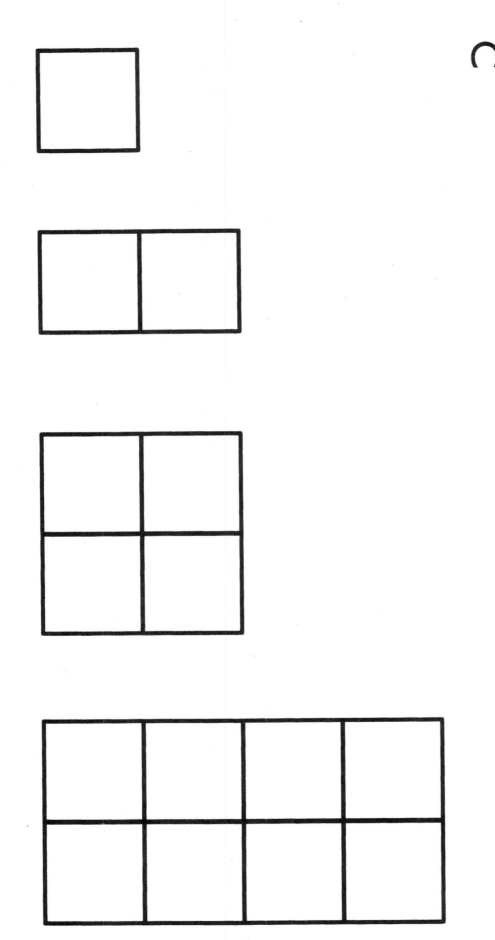

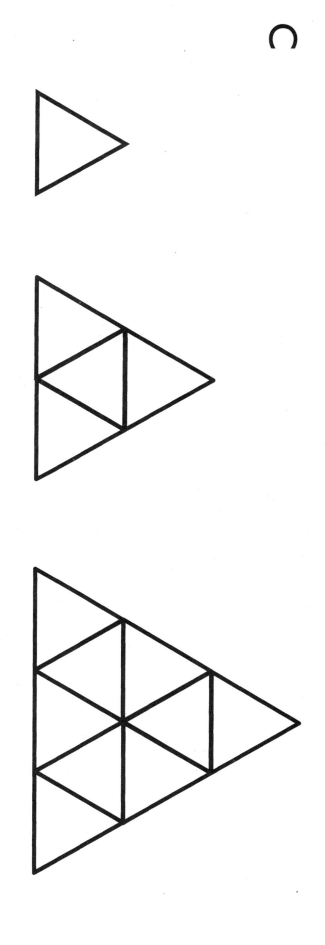

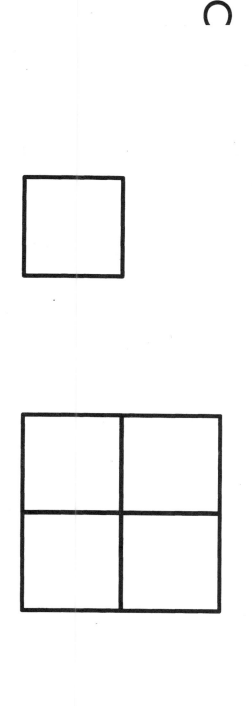

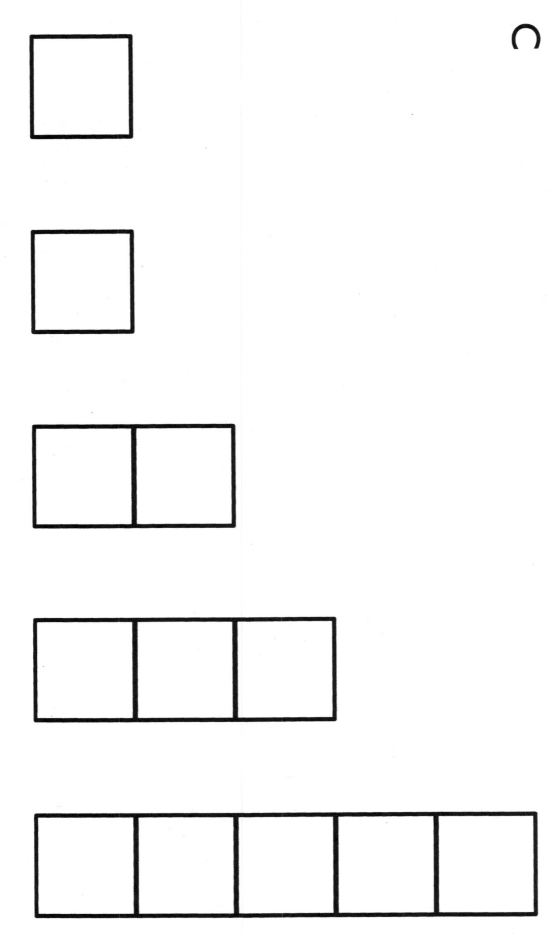

C

Activity 7: Tessellations

Overview

Tessellations in their simplest form are tilings, like those your students are familiar with in their homes. In fact, the word *tessellation* comes from the Latin *tessella*, which means small square stone or tile. However, for a tiling to be a tessellation, three things are necessary: (1) There are no gaps between shapes; (2) There are no overlays of tiles on top of or over one another; and (3) There is a pattern of one or more shapes that repeats itself and can be extended in the plane.

In this activity, students are given cards with tessellations on them. The students use pattern blocks to cover the tiling on the card. They then attempt to continue building the tessellation so it fills the entire card. Students can also use the pattern blocks to create their own tessellations. They can look for examples of tessellations in bathroom and kitchen tilings, architectural designs, quilting, art forms, and nature after building tessellations with pattern blocks.

Tessellations connect to mathematics in many ways. Beyond direct connections to geometry and pattern, these tilings lend themselves to a study of dimension and area. Tessellations also connect mathematics to history and art. Both regular geometric shapes and amorphic (non-regular) shapes lend themselves to beautiful design work. On page 202 of the "Behind the Scenes" section, we have included some additional cultural and historical background on tessellations.

Set this activity up at one or more stations and let students explore at their own pace *or* follow the steps listed on page 145 to introduce the activity to the entire class prior to having them work at the stations.

> ### Tessellation Jingle
>
> Build tessellations, bit by bit,
> Repeating patterns, perfect fit,
> Like checkerboards or bathroom tiles
> Make patterns stretch for miles and miles—
> Remember: There can be no gap,
> All shapes must fit, not overlap.

What You Need For One Station

- ❒ 6 tessellation pattern cards on card stock
- ❒ 1 set of pattern blocks
- ❒ (*optional*) 1 Tessellations sign
- ❒ (*optional*) white card stock

*As an alternative to regular pattern blocks, there are also **rainbow** pattern blocks that lend themselves nicely to this activity. See "Sources for Materials" on page 213 .*

Getting Ready

1. Decide how many Tessellations stations you intend to set up.

2. Duplicate the appropriate tessellation pattern cards from masters on pages 150–165 on white card stock. As desired, laminate or cover the cards with clear contact paper for greater durability. The simplest patterns are labeled with an "A."

3. Place the tessellation pattern cards with a set of pattern blocks at each station. For this activity, stations must be **flat**. Use the floor if your desks or table tops are slanted.

4. If you are using signs, duplicate one Tessellations sign from page 149 for each station.

5. Read "Special Considerations" and decide if you want to present a pre-activity to your students.

6. Just before presenting the activity, gather one of the simpler tessellation cards and the pattern blocks needed to build it.

Special Considerations

Many students have difficulty differentiating between designs and tessellations. It is helpful to introduce actual examples of tessellations to them, either before or after they build in this activity. It may also be helpful to remind students of the differences between a tessellation and other designs, by pointing out that for a design to be a tessellation it must have a repeating pattern of the same shape (or shapes) with no gaps and no overlaps.

A bee honeycomb (constructed with hexagonal shapes) is an example of a tessellation from the natural world. A checkerboard is another example of a tessellation. Samples of tiling from a hardware store may spark students to look in their homes for other examples. A walk in the school neighborhood can provide examples of both tessellations and designs.

For young students, the concept of a tessellation is sophisticated. However, experiences with this activity will provide a focus on patterns, which is highly appropriate for primary students. For older students, this activity will provide experiences with advanced patterns and at least an intuitive understanding of tessellations that can be explored in greater depth in later grades.

Introducing Tessellations to the Entire Class

1. Ask students to define a pattern. [A student may point to a stripe pattern on her shirt, such as: purple, magenta, purple, magenta. Or she may look at the classroom calendar to point out a repeating pattern.] Define a pattern as anything that repeats itself over and over.

2. Ask if anyone knows what a tessellation is. After listening to some responses, explain that a tessellation is a tiling. Ask students if and where they have ever seen tilings. [Answers may include in bathroom showers, kitchen counters, tiled floors, swimming pools, etc.]

3. Hold up the tessellation card. Explain that it is also a tessellation. Elaborate on the definition of a tessellation to include the fact that there are no gaps between shapes and no overlays of one shape on top of another. In addition, tell them that a tessellation is a repeating pattern. If the Tessellation Jingle from page 143 is appropriate for your students, read it out loud or put it on the board. Ask students to describe the repeating pattern on the card.

4. Tell students that they will cover or "tile" the card with pattern blocks. Begin putting pattern blocks on the card. As you do so, draw attention to the pattern by saying things like: "Notice how there's a green triangle at the top of each yellow hexagon." Cover all the pattern block shapes on the card with real pattern blocks.

5. Ask older students how to extend the pattern. Extend on one or two of the sides to demonstrate.

6. Have students go to stations and create tessellations using the skill-appropriate cards.

7. As students are building their tessellations on the pattern cards, circulate and ask them to point out the pattern. Encourage them to continue the tessellation in every direction off the pattern card.

Looking for patterns develops logical thinking and the ability to predict future events. As the mind searches for patterns, sense can be made from what may at first appear to be discrete, separate, and unrelated things or events. Patterns are also found in nature and life cycles. The search for, discovery, and analysis of patterns is extremely important in math, science, and many other fields.

Going Further

1. **Designer Tessellations!** Tell students that they are interior designers and their job is to come up with a color scheme for a bathroom or kitchen. Give them a tessellation master to color in, according to their own décor. *Tessellation Teaching Masters* by Dale Seymour is one good source for these masters. Younger students can simply color in the tessellation masters with your assistance, so they maintain a color pattern.

2. **Regular Tessellations**: Have students use only one of the pattern block shapes to see if they can tile the plane with that shape. For example, start with the square. Does it tessellate? [Yes, in fact, all the pattern block shapes tessellate.] Can you make it tessellate in more than one way? Next, explore the other three quadrilaterals—the blue parallelogram, the tan parallelogram, and the red trapezoid. Do each of these shapes tessellate? Without actually using the triangle and the hexagon, can students predict or prove that these shapes will tessellate? This is an early form of a geometric proof done concretely! Students can provide a variety of proofs such as, "Since a blue parallelogram can be made with two triangles and we discovered that the parallelograms tessellate, then the triangle can also tessellate."

3. **Great Debate**: Review the definition of a tessellation and then allow students to use any combination of pattern blocks to create their own unique tessellations. After they are done, have the class walk around to each table of creations. Ask the students who *did not* build it to say whether or not each creation is a tessellation or a design. Be sure they can explain their thinking and find the repeating pattern in the tessellation! This will help students distinguish tessellations from intricate design.

4. **Tessellating Classroom Materials!** Many materials in your classroom lend themselves to creating tessellations. For example, a set of dominoes, a deck of cards, or even a stack of index cards can be used. Encourage students to come up with other possible materials keeping in mind that the materials need to be all the same shape and size.

5. **Tessellating Quadrilaterals!** Investigate the ability of any four-sided polygon to tessellate. Begin with small rectangular index cards. Can students make them tessellate? Trace around the rectangle on a sheet

of paper to record the tessellation. Now transform the rectangle into a square by cutting it. Test its ability to tessellate. Again, record the tessellation on a sheet of paper. Now, have students alter the card so that there are still four sides. Using this shape, can students create a tessellation on a sheet of paper as they did with the rectangle and the square?

6. **The Art of Tessellation!** Show examples of art-related tessellations throughout history. (See the Special Note on Tessellations on page 202.) Have students research and present one aspect of tessellations as an art form.

7. **M.C. Escher**: This Dutch artist was a master at altering geometric shapes and creating tessellating forms such as birds, reptiles, fish, and people. Escher translated, rotated, and reflected shapes to create more unusual tessellations. He also incorporated optical illusions in his work. Students can create Escher-style tessellations by altering shapes. The following is an example of how to alter a square.

How to Create an Escher-like Shape from a Square

a. Start with a card stock square.

b. Shade the front of the square so that students can easily tell the difference between front and back.

c. Cut a piece out from *one side* of the square only! Cut from corner to corner. The cut can be angular or curvy. Caution students not to cut too close to the opposite side.

d. Slide the cut-out piece to the opposite side and tape it on. (Be sure the shaded side is facing up!)

e. Using the same procedure as in step c, cut out another piece from either of the two sides that have not been altered in any way! (Be sure that when this next cut is made, you do not cut into the attached piece.)

f. Slide the cut-out piece to the opposite side and tape it down. Again be sure you have the shaded pieces all facing up.

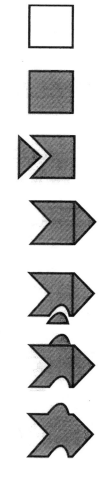

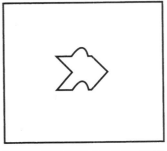

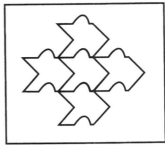

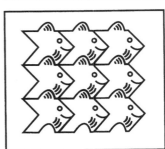

g. Look at your shape and see what it looks like! Rotate your altered shape to inspire different possibilities. For example, in one direction the shape may look like a frog while at another angle it may look like a fish. Decide which way you want to orient your shape. Place it in the center of a piece of paper. Trace around the outline of your shape.

h. Next slide your shape above the traced one. It should fit the first tracing like a puzzle piece. Then trace the shape again. Now slide the shape below and again fit the shape in and trace. Continue by fitting the shape to the right and left of the original traced shape. This new shape still tessellates because the original square shape tessellates. This alteration (a slide transformation of the square) maintains the tessellation.

i. Continue to trace your shape in the same manner until the paper is filled. Decorate! What does this tessellation look like to you?

"Day and Night" by M.C.Escher, © M.C. Escher Heirs c/o Cordon Art, Baarn, Holland. Courtesy of Vorpal Galleries: San Francisco and New York City.

Tessellations

Tessellations in their simplest form are tilings.
For a tiling with geometric shapes to be a tessellation:
1. There must be a **clear pattern**;
2. There are **no gaps** between shapes; and
3. There are **no overlays**.

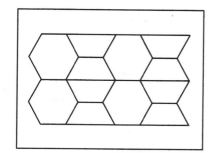

1. Choose a tessellation pattern to tile.

2. Use pattern blocks to cover the pattern.

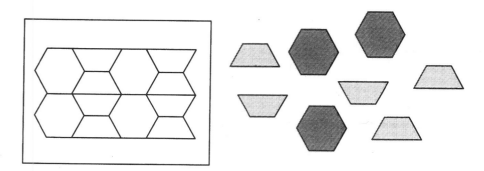

3. Extend the pattern until the entire card—and beyond—is covered with pattern blocks.

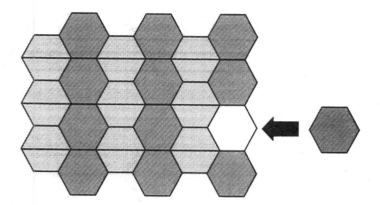

4. Create a tessellation of your own!

A

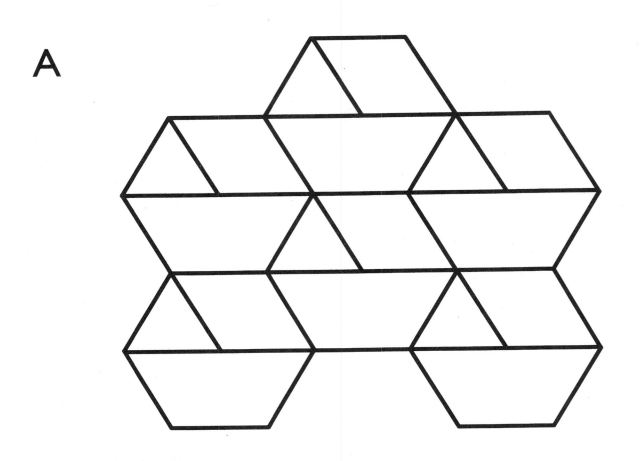

A

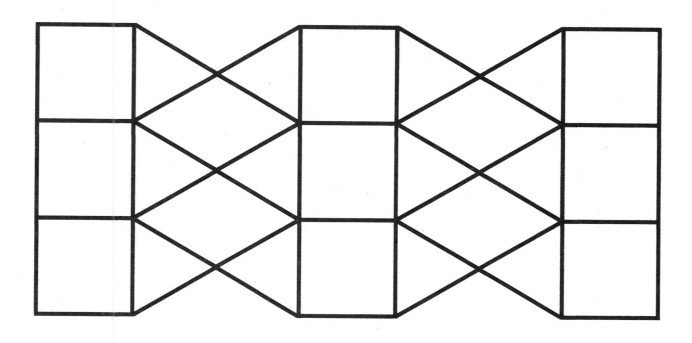

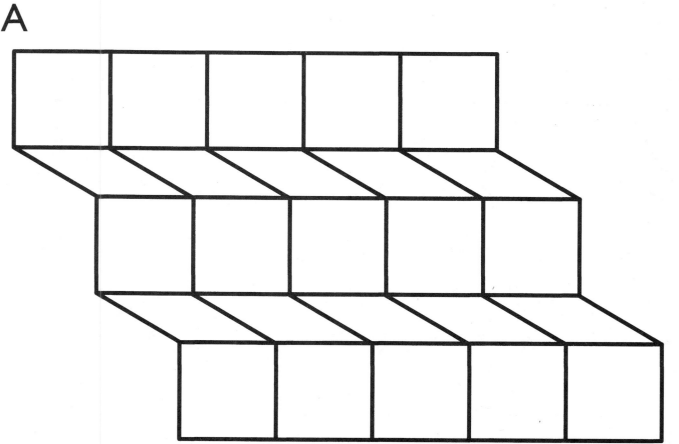

A

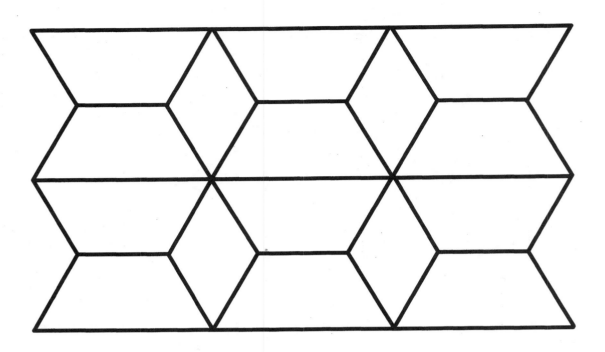

A

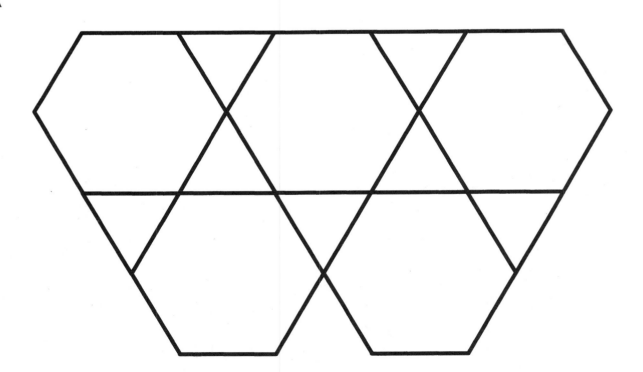

A

A

A

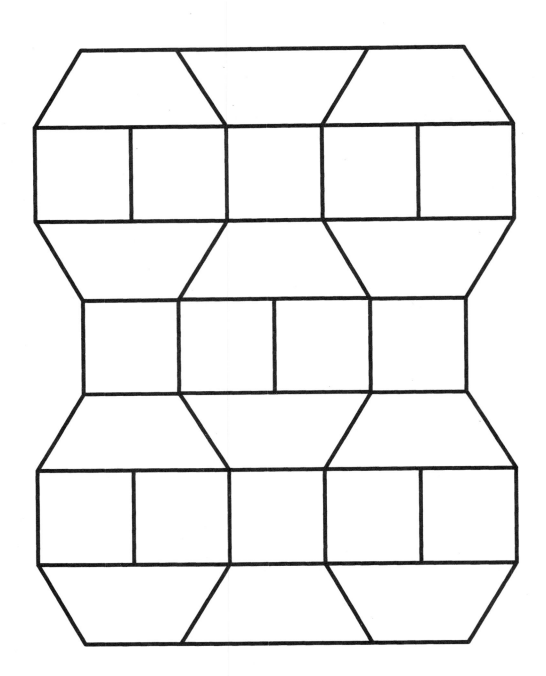

A

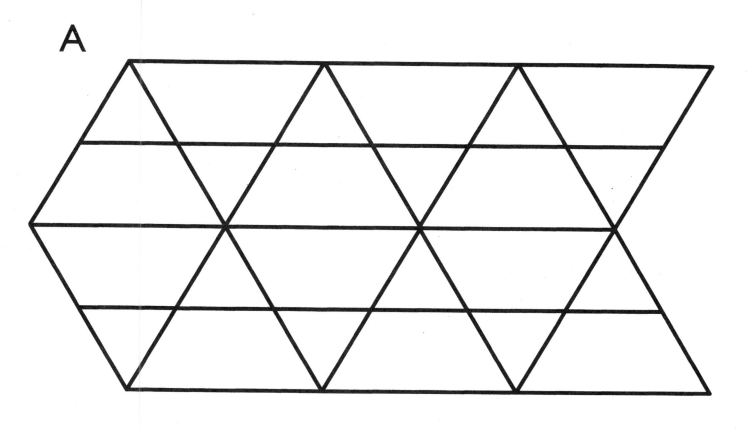

A

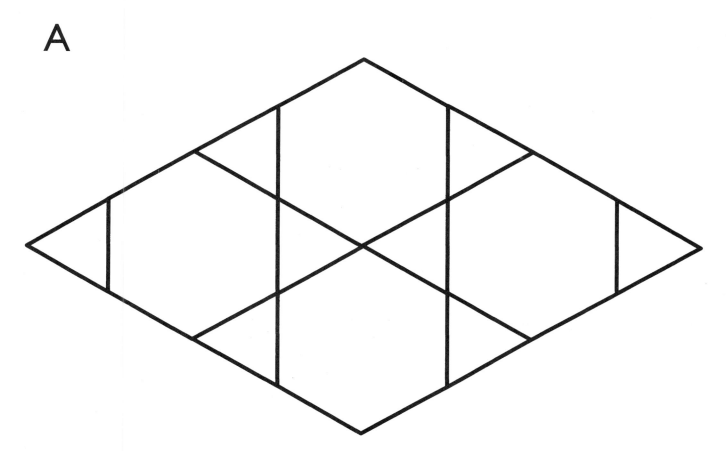

B

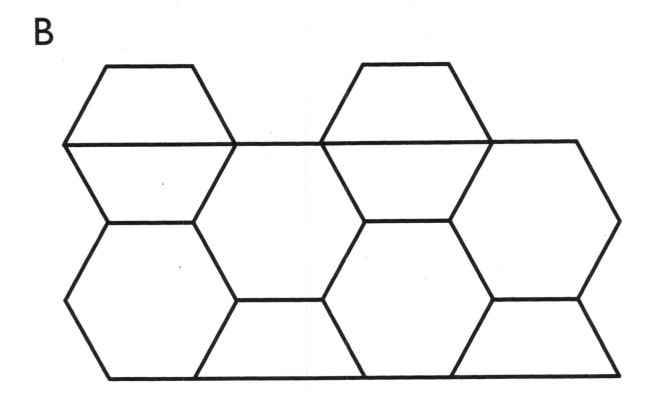

B

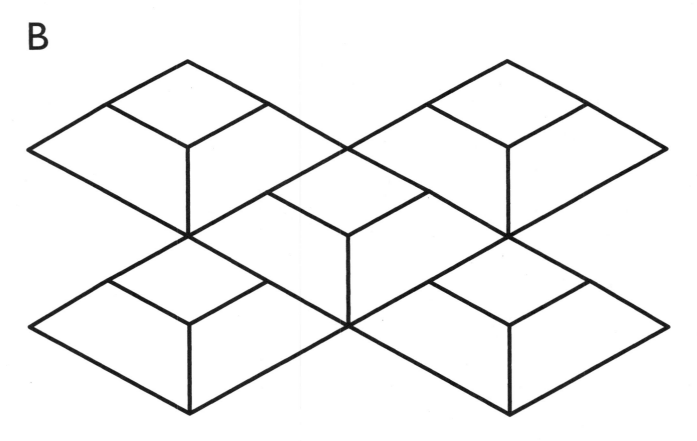

B

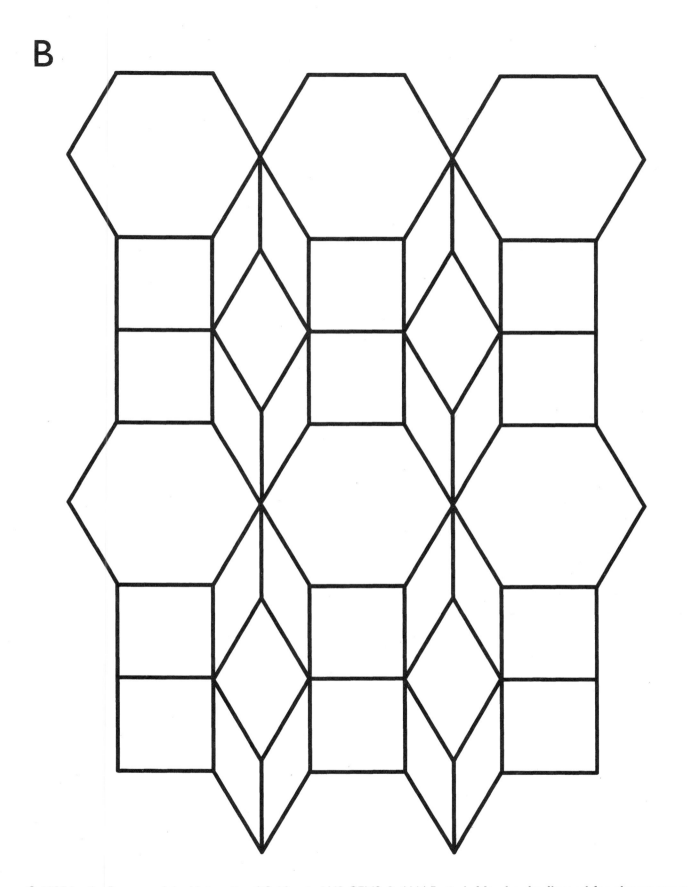

B

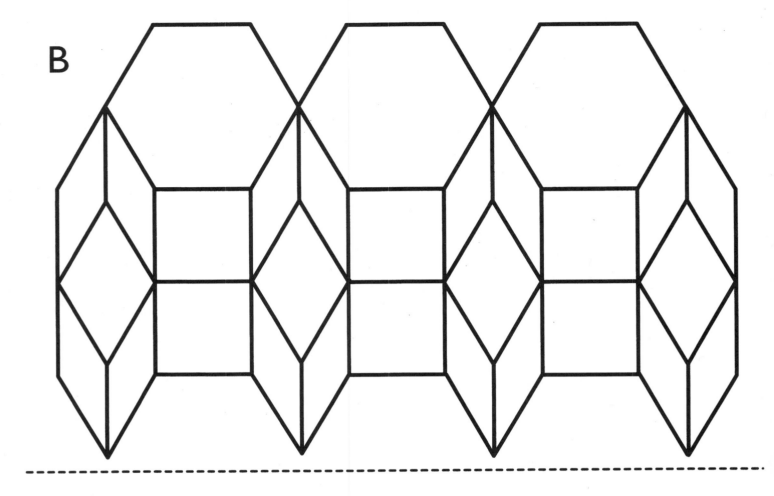

B

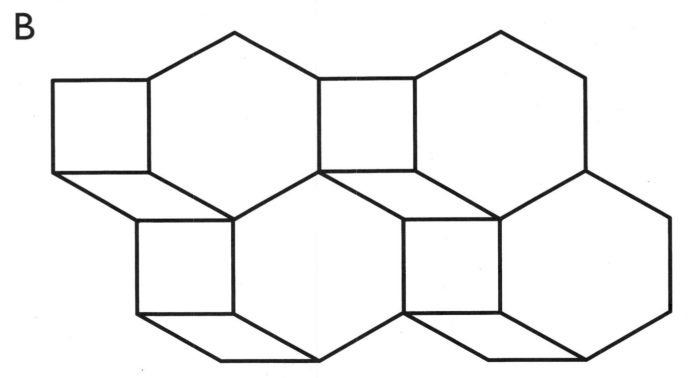

C

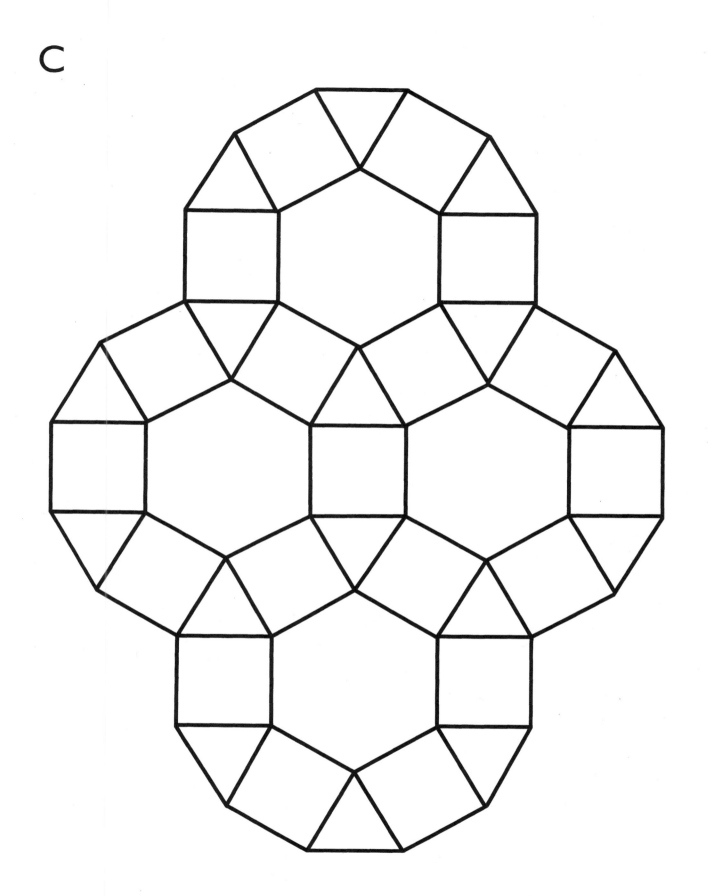

C

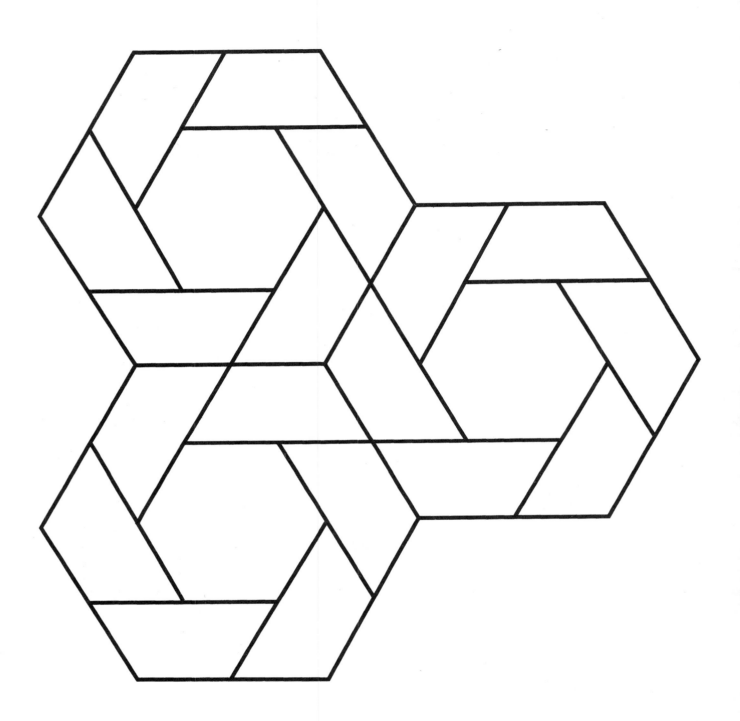

C

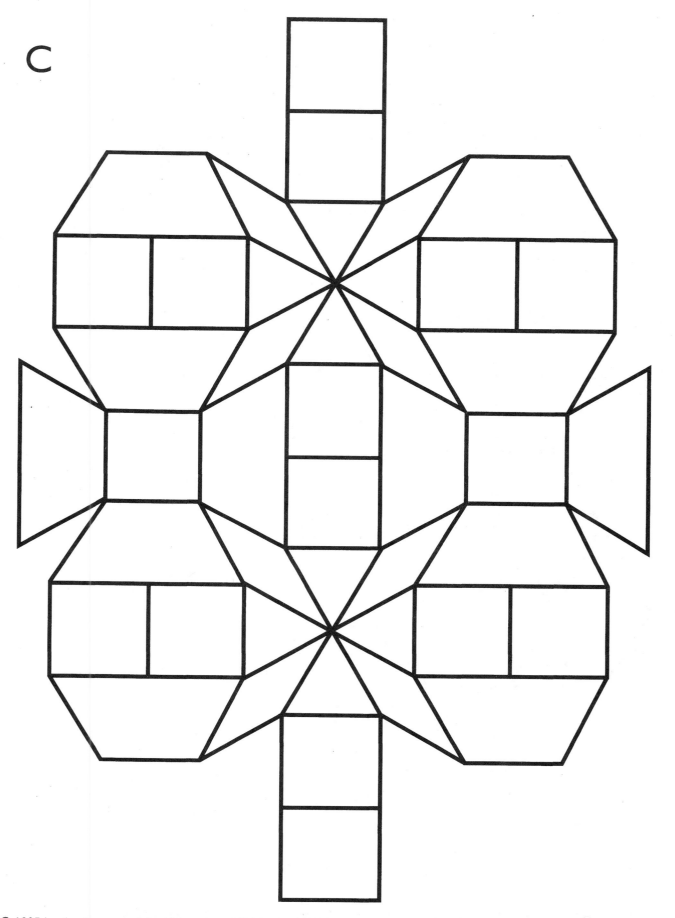

C

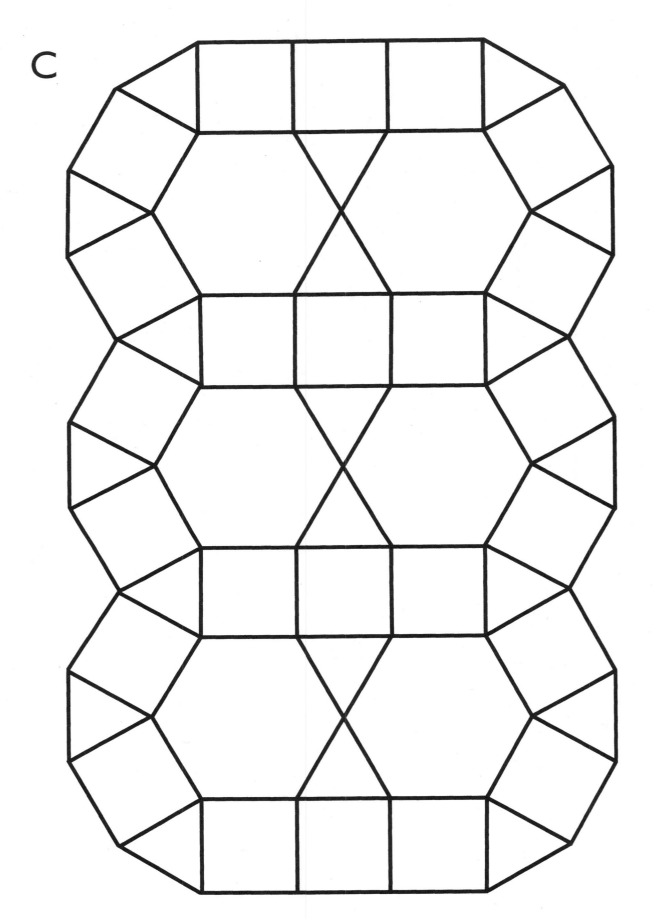

C

Activity 8: Tangrams

Overview

An ancient Chinese tale provides one explanation for the origin of tangrams. The story has it that a skilled artisan made a beautiful square tile for the Emperor. On his way to deliver the tile, it fell and broke into seven pieces! The distressed artist asked for help to get it back together again. The first person was able to make a rectangle out of the seven pieces. Another person was able to make a triangle. Still another made a parallelogram. Finally, the tile was pieced together, back into its original square shape, and presented to the Emperor. To this day, the seven pieces that made the tile square are still used as a puzzle known as a tangram.

The seven pieces of the tangram puzzle are called "tans," and include the following geometric shapes: two large triangles, one medium triangle, two small triangles, one parallelogram, and one square. These seven pieces can create a square, as well as other geometric shapes and forms.

In this activity, students make their own tangrams. They create sets of the seven tans either by cutting out a set of shapes from a master or by following directions on how to fold and cut a square sheet of paper. Before attempting to re-create the square, students have opportunities to create animals, letters, vehicles, buildings, designs, and their own unique images with the tans.

At the end of this activity there are many "Going Further" activities that invite students to use the tans for further geometric explorations. For example, young students can build various polygons and learn their geometric names. For more information on polygons, see page 197 of "Behind the Scenes." Using only three small shapes (such as the square and two triangles), they can see how many other geometric shapes they can make. Students can also record many different ways of building the same shape, such as a hexagon with a prescribed number of tans. Older students can investigate these properties as well as delve further into polygons with more sides. In addition, they

Small plastic tangrams can also be used instead of their own sets of tangrams. In addition, a set of giant-size tangrams is helpful to teach the shapes and solutions to problems posed. A source for both small plastic tangrams and the giant-size set is listed in the "Sources for Materials" section on page 213. Alternately, you may want to make your own large set out of a sheet of tagboard.

In this book, Grandfather Tang tells about two shape-changing fox fairies who try to outdo each other until a hunter brings danger to both of them. The seven shapes ("tans") that grandfather uses to tell the story are the pieces of an ancient Chinese tangram puzzle. As you read to your class, your students can use clues in the story to predict how the foxes will transform before the animal is revealed. After the story, students can use the tans to investigate and explore geometry.

can investigate congruence and similarity in geometric shapes.

Set this activity up at one or more stations and let students explore at their own pace *or* follow the steps listed on page 169 to introduce the activity to the entire class prior to having them work at the stations.

What You Need For One Station

- ❏ 6 tangram masters **OR**
  6 square sheets of colored paper
- ❏ 6 scissors
- ❏ 1 large square of paper
- ❏ (*optional*) 6 sheets of colored paper
- ❏ (*optional*) 6 glue sticks
- ❏ (*optional*) 6 envelopes to hold shapes **OR**
  6 paper clips to hold shapes
- ❏ (*optional*) 1 Tangram sign

Getting Ready

1. Decide how many Tangram stations you intend to set up.

2. Decide if you will use the book, *Grandfather Tang's Story: A Tale Told with Tangrams*, by Ann Tompert, to introduce tangrams to the children. Obtain a copy and read the story ahead of time. Making this outstanding "literature connection" is highly recommended!

3. Decide whether or not your students will cut their tangram shapes out of the pre-printed master sheet or out of a square sheet of paper. Older students (those in second grade and above) are capable of cutting out tangram shapes from a blank sheet. Although this is more difficult and time-consuming, it has educational benefits (see sidebar on the next page).

   a. For younger or less experienced students, duplicate the tangram master on page 181. You may want to duplicate it in six different colors so that each student at the station has a different colored set of shapes. This helps students to distinguish their own set of tangrams and avoids students confusing their shapes with one another. Cut a large set of tangrams out of a 12" x 12" sheet of construction paper. This set is for demonstration purposes when students share tangram discoveries.

b. For older or more experienced students, cut 8 ½" x 8 ½" squares out of six different colored sheets of 8 ½" x 11" paper. At each station, put one square sheet of each of the six different colors. This helps students to distinguish their own set of tangrams and avoids students confusing their shapes with one another. Make a large (at least 11" x 11") square sheet of paper to model how to make tangrams.

4. If you are using signs, duplicate the appropriate Tangrams station sign from pages 182–187 for each station.

5. Decide if your students will glue their set of tangrams onto a sheet of paper to record one shape or design that they created with the tangrams or if they will store the tangrams for later use.

- If they will be gluing down their favorite tangram creations, have available six sheets of paper of a contrasting color to the colored shapes, along with glue sticks.

- If they will be saving the shapes, have envelopes or paper clips available to keep the sets together.

6. Set up stations around the room with the materials appropriate to the way that your students will explore tangrams.

Introducing Tangrams to the Entire Class

1. (*Optional*) Read *Grandfather Tang's Story: A Tale Told with Tangrams* to your students.

2. Model how to create a set of tangrams, according to whichever of the two versions below is appropriate, the first (Version 1) for students who will make their own tangrams from a master (see page 181), and the second (Version 2) for students who will make tangrams from a square sheet of paper.

There is great value in students creating their own tangrams. Through doing so, students have the concrete knowledge that they began with a square, from which they created the other shapes (tans). In addition, as they cut shapes from the square, they are using geometric vocabulary while making geometric observations and discoveries. Sophisticated concepts such as non-regular geometric shapes, congruence, and similarity can be introduced using these versatile math manipulatives.

Version 1: For students who are going to make their tangrams from a master

1. Hold up a master sheet. Ask what large shape is on the sheet. [Square]

2. Demonstrate how to cut out the square first and then the remaining shapes.

3. Count the number of shapes. Identify them. [2 large triangles, 1 medium triangle, 2 small triangles, 1 square, 1 parallelogram]

4. Ask for ideas on what could be made with the tangrams.

5. Have children go to the stations and cut out the seven shapes (tans) from the master sheet. Allow children time to freely explore the tans.

6. Encourage students to use their tans to create something, such as a real or imaginary animal or creature, a letter of the alphabet or a number, a building or vehicle, or a design.

7. After students have had an opportunity to freely explore the tans, explore the geometry of tangrams. Ask how many shapes they have. [7] What shapes are they? [triangles, square, parallelogram] Have them find the largest shape and the smallest shape.

8. Next, ask students to organize their shapes in some way. Have several students share their sorting methods. [Answers may include: into triangles and quadrilaterals; sizes of tans; size and shape of tans; etc.]

Some teachers have had the children cut out the tangram master in a similar fashion as the older students cut out a plain square. The lines on the master enable students to follow directions and cut lines accurately. Alternately, for those children who are not yet skilled at cutting a straight line, some teachers have sets of either plastic or pre-cut paper tangrams available.

If you have read the story, encourage students to create their own animals out of the tans. Allow time for students to see the variety of animals that were created and to guess what each others' animals are. You may want to have children record their animals for parents and posterity, by gluing tans onto a sheet of paper that is a contrasting color. At another time, students can also write a story about their animal or write clues so others can guess what their animals are.

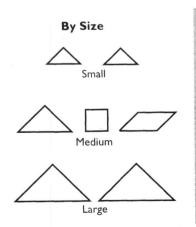

By Shape	By Size	By Number of Sides
Triangles	Small	Triangles
	Medium	
Square Parallelogram	Large	Quadrilaterals

9. Have all students separate out the triangles. How many triangles are there? [5] Put them in size order. Have students set aside the two large triangles. Using just the medium triangle and the two small triangles, ask what shapes they can make. At first, students may make pine trees, sailboats, crowns, and other real-world items. It is important that they have the opportunity to do so.

10. Guide the children into making geometric shapes with the three triangles. Ask if they can make a rectangle. After someone has been successful, let them demonstrate how to make it with your large demonstration set of tangrams. Be sure all students can create a rectangle. Next, ask if they can create a square. Again, have a student demonstrate the solution. Continue with additional shapes, such as triangle, parallelogram, trapezoid, pentagon, etc., depending on your students abilities and interest. (See page 187 for more geometric explorations.)

Some teachers have waited to begin the geometric exploration until a second class period. Other teachers have begun the geometric exploration as soon as students have cut out their tans and then ended the period with a creative building time with tans.

TANGRAMS

I picked some "TANS" up with great care

then placed one here, or maybe there,

I tried and tried, and pulled my hair,

but then at last—I made a SQUARE !

Version 2: For students who are going to make their tangrams from a square sheet of paper

1. Tell students you are going to help them turn a square into a seven-piece tangram puzzle. Be sure students stay at your pace. Have students go to stations and have a square sheet of paper and scissors ready.

2. Use the following step-by-step instructions to model how to make a set of tangrams using a large sheet of square paper:

> a. Fold the square sheet of paper in half on the diagonal so that two triangles are formed. Crease the paper. Open the paper. Look at the fold line inside of the square. Ask what type of line they have created. [diagonal] Ask if there are any other possible diagonals in the square. [yes, one] Cut along the diagonal (crease). What shapes have you created? [two triangles] What do you know about these triangles? [right triangles, isosceles, congruent]

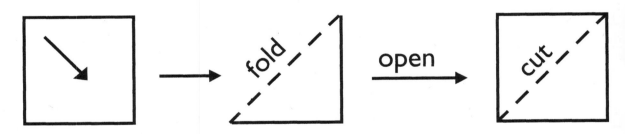

Have students make the original square out of the two triangles. Ask questions, such as:

Can they make another triangle out of the two triangles?
Can they make a parallelogram?

b. Take one of the triangles and fold it in half to form two congruent triangles. Be sure the corners line up when you fold the paper. Crease the paper. Open and cut along the crease line.

Pose questions and challenges, such as:

What are the two shapes created by cutting the triangle? [two triangles]
Are they congruent? [yes]
Use the three triangles to make the original square.
What other shapes can they make? [triangle, parallelogram, rectangle, trapezoid]

c. Set aside the two smaller triangles. Take the larger triangle. You can refer to it as a "mountain" shape. Match the opposite vertices but **DO NOT CREASE!** Pinch the middle of the paper to mark the midpoint of the mountain's base. Then open up the triangle. Take the mountain and fold its "peak" down to the midpoint. Crease the paper. A small triangle and a trapezoid will be formed. Open the crease. Cut along the crease line.

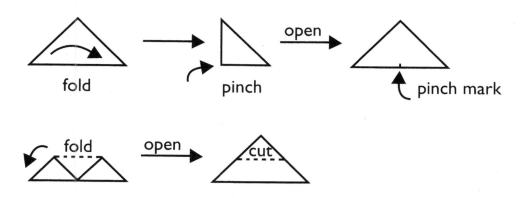

Ask questions, such as:

What shapes are created? [a triangle and a trapezoid]
What shape other than a triangle can you make using those two shapes? [parallelogram, hexagon]

d. Take the trapezoid. Fold it in half so that the small angles meet. You can refer to this shape as a "shoe," so that the next steps will be easier for students to follow. Open and cut along the crease line.

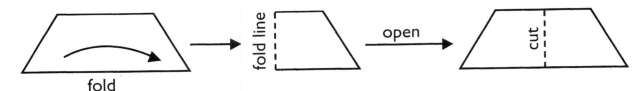

fold   fold line   open   cut

Pose the following questions:

How many "shoe" shapes do you have? [2]
How many sides does the "shoe" shape have? [4]
What is another name for a four-sided shape? [quadrilateral]
What is another name for this quadrilateral? [trapezoid. A trapezoid is a quadrilateral with only one pair of parallel sides.]
Using the two quadrilaterals, make a pentagon.
Using the triangle and the two quadrilaterals, what other shapes can you make? [square, parallelogram, pentagon, hexagon, heptagon, octagon]

e. Take one of the shoe shapes. Take the "toe" of the shoe and fold it so that it will touch the "heel." A square and a triangle should be formed. Make a crease. Open up and cut apart the two shapes.

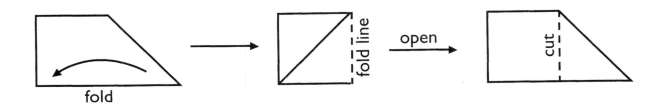

fold   fold line   open   cut

f. Take the other shoe shape. This time take the "heel" and have it touch the top of the "laces." Now a triangle and a parallelogram will be formed. Crease the paper. Open and cut.

3. Explain to your students that these seven pieces are the tans of the tangram puzzle—five triangles, a square, and a parallelogram.

4. Have students put their initials on all seven pieces (tans).

5. Give students an opportunity to freely create shapes and forms with their tans. If you have read the story, encourage students to create their own animals out of the tans. Allow time for students to see the variety of animals that were created and to guess each others' animals. Then, you may want to have children record one of their animals by gluing tans onto a sheet of paper that is a contrasting color. Students can also write a story about their animal or write clues for others to guess which animal they created.

6. If students will not be gluing their shapes to create animals, you may want to end this class period by challenging students to re-make the original square with their seven pieces.

Going Further

1. **Tangram Animals** from *Grandfather Tang's Story*: Copy and enlarge the two fox fairies from the story and have students use tangram pieces to make them. Additionally, copy and enlarge the other animals from the story so that students can also make these animals.

2. **Create a Puzzle**: Have students develop tangram puzzles. First make a shape with the tangram pieces, then draw the around the perimeter (edges) of the shape. Challenge classmates to solve the puzzle by using their seven tans to cover the shape!

3. **Design A Tile**: Just as the artisan in the ancient Chinese tale made a beautiful tile, have students create a beautiful square tile. Give each student a Tangram Master from page 181 and have them cut out the square. On the side *without* lines, have students design a fancy tile. Then they can cut out the tans using the lines on the undecorated side. Other students can try to put their classmates' tiles back together again!

4. **More Geometric Explorations**

   a. **Identifying and Creating Shapes**: Have your students work with their tangrams on any or all of the following geometric explorations according to their abilities. Each one is likely to take a full class period. At whatever point your students need to end their exploration, have them put their shapes into an envelope or hold them together with a paper clip, so they will be ready for more geometric activities next time. (If students glued their shapes to create animals, duplicate the Tangram Master from page 181 so they can cut out a new set of tans to use for these activities.)

      1.) **Identifying Shapes**: Have young students identify and name the three shapes: triangles, square, and parallelogram. Review the characteristics of each shape. Look for items in the classroom that are similar in shape.

2.) **Creating Shapes with Tans:** Have your students use their tans to create polygons. See if any patterns or strategies evolve as they work with the tans.

a.) Use the two small triangles to make: a triangle, a square, and a parallelogram.

b.) What shapes can be made using the *two small triangles* and the:

- *square?* [rectangle, triangle, trapezoid, parallelogram]

- *parallelogram?* [rectangle, triangle, trapezoid, parallelogram]

- *medium triangle?* [rectangle, square, parallelogram, trapezoid, triangle]

Note: Other non-regular shapes can also be formed. An exploration of non-regular shapes is suggested below.

3.) Use the two small triangles, the medium triangle, and one large triangle to make the following: a square, a rectangle, a triangle, a parallelogram, a trapezoid, and a non-regular quadrilateral.

4.) Remove the two large triangles, and use the five remaining tans to make the following: triangle, square, parallelogram, trapezoids, rectangle, non-regular quadrilateral.

b. **Non-Regular Geometric Shapes:** Often students equate quadrilaterals with their more common forms, such as rectangles, squares, parallelograms, rhombi, and trapezoids. However, by definition, a quadrilateral is any closed figure with four sides and four angles. The tans can help students broaden their thinking not only about quadrilaterals but also about other polygons that are commonly seen in their regular forms.

1.) Start with an exploration of quadrilaterals. Have students define a quadrilateral.

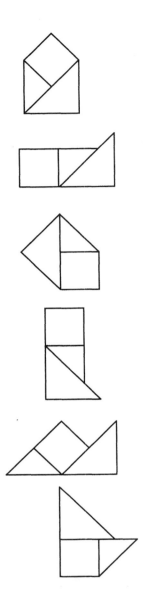

Pentagons

List the quadrilaterals they know. Tell students that they are now going to create non-regular quadrilaterals. Have them use any of their tans to create a quadrilateral other than the ones they listed. Have students share their results. Ask if this was a challenging task? Why or why not?

2.) Next, explore pentagons (which are closed polygons with five sides). Ask students to draw a pentagon. Ask where pentagons are seen in the real world? [home plate in baseball] For starters, have all students work with the same three shapes, for example, the two small triangles and the medium triangle *or* one small triangle, the square, and the medium triangle. Have students record their pentagons either by tracing around the shapes or by gluing the shapes on a sheet of paper. How many different pentagons did they make?

Note: If students glue their pentagons, you may want to have many copies of the Tangram Master available so they can record several pentagons.

3.) Students can continue to explore other possible ways to create pentagons using other tans. Recording their findings will help students expand the idea of what a pentagon is.

4.) Students can continue to create other non-regular polygons with the tans, such as hexagons and octagons—i.e., the shape of a stop sign—that we usually see in their regular forms. Students who are ready for a challenge may want to explore heptagons or nonegons. (See the Geometric Glossary in the "Behind the Scenes" section for more information about polygons.)

c. **Congruent Shapes**: Ask students what they know about congruent shapes. For a concrete example, have students take the two large triangles. Place one triangle flat on the table. Then place the other triangle directly on top of it. Ask questions, such as: Does it fit exactly on it? Do they have the same shape? Are they the same size? If any two shapes are identical in size and shape, they are congruent. Are there any other shapes in the set of tans that are congruent? [small triangles]

1.) Have students select a tan such as the square. Can they create a congruent square using other tans? What tans did they use to make the square? [two small triangles]

Note: Younger students can be directed to use the two small triangles to build right on top of the square. This will clearly illustrate congruence.

2.) Can a congruent parallelogram be built? [Yes, with two small triangles. Again have younger students build directly on top of the parallelogram.]

3.) Can they build a congruent medium triangle more than one way? [No, only one way, again with two triangles.]

4.) How many congruent large triangles can be made using more than one shape? [There are three ways: two small triangles and square; two small triangles and parallelogram; and two small triangles and medium triangle.]

Note: The configuration of the shapes may be different, but these are only three combinations of shape that can create the large triangle.

d. **Similar Shapes:** To help your students concretely understand the definition of similar triangles, have them use two triangles from the tangrams—one of the small triangles and the medium triangle.

Hold the small triangle in one hand and the medium one in the opposite hand. (*Hint:* It is easiest to hold the small one in the hand with which you write.)

Hold the smallest triangle up in front of (about four inches from) one eye. Then hold the other triangle behind the small triangle further away from your eye until the small triangle lines up exactly to cover the larger triangle. Tell students that these triangles are similar. Then ask how students would define what similar shapes are. [They both have the same shape and angle measure, but the lengths of the sides are different—either proportionally larger or smaller.] Agree on a student definition for the term "similar."

Ask if any tangram shapes are similar. Be sure to have students explain their thinking. Challenge them to:

1.) Start with the triangles. Are all three triangles similar? Why? How many other similar triangles can they make with the tans?

2.) Next use the square tan. Make similar squares. How many can be made? What tans were used?

3.) Make a parallelogram that is slightly bigger than the parallelogram in the tangram set. What tans were used? Make the largest parallelogram possible. What tans were used?

e. **Challenges?** Have students set aside the two large triangles. Have them make a triangle using the remaining five tans. Finally, have students use all seven tans to make a square.

Tangram Master

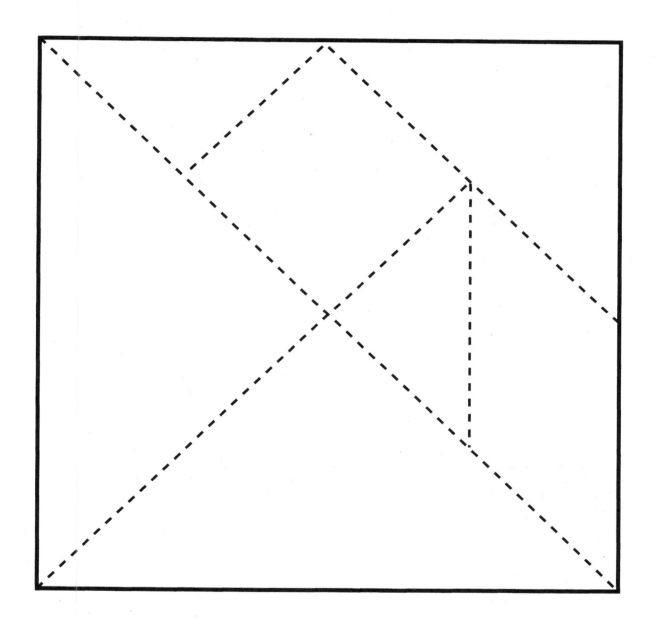

Tangrams

1 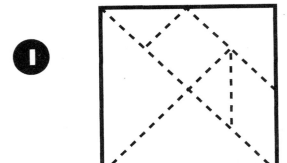 Take a tangram master.

2 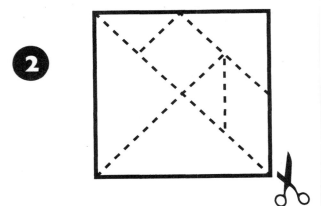 Cut out the shapes along all the lines.

3 Make sure you have all seven pieces cut out:

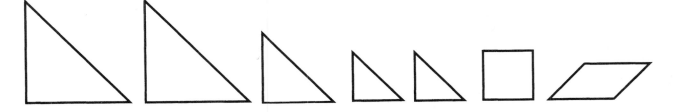

4 Can you make an animal or creature?

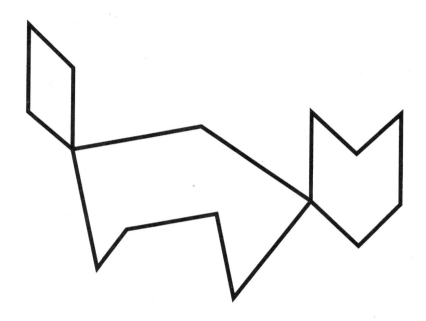

5 Can you make a letter of the alphabet?

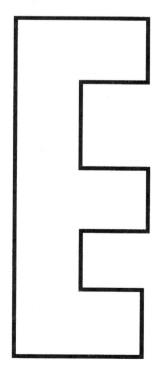

Tangrams

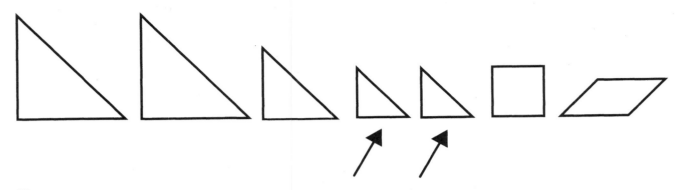

1 Take the 2 small triangles.

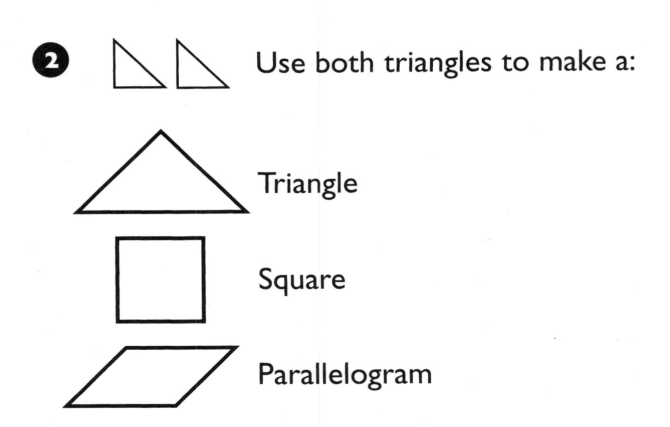

2 Use both triangles to make a:

Triangle

Square

Parallelogram

Tangrams

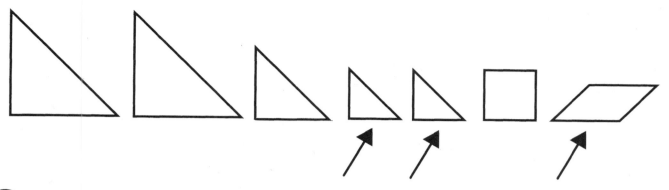

1 Take the 2 small triangles and the parallelogram.

2 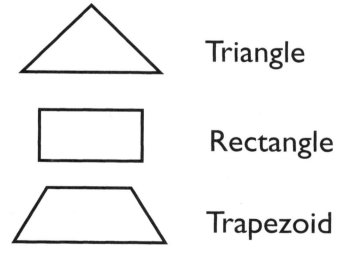 Use both triangles and the parallelogram to make a:

Triangle

Rectangle

Trapezoid

Parallelogram

Tangrams

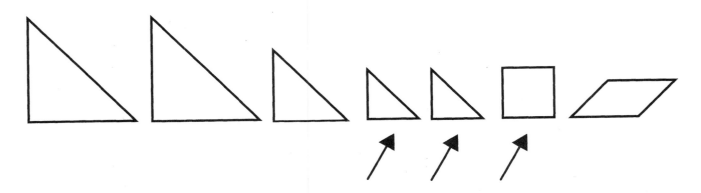

1 Take the 2 small triangles and the square.

2 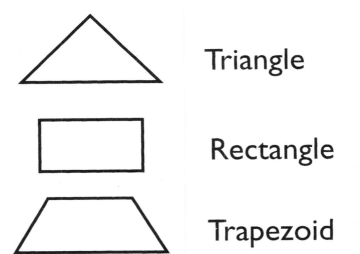 Use both triangles and the square to make a:

Triangle

Rectangle

Trapezoid

Parallelogram

Tangrams

1 Use all 7 pieces to make a:

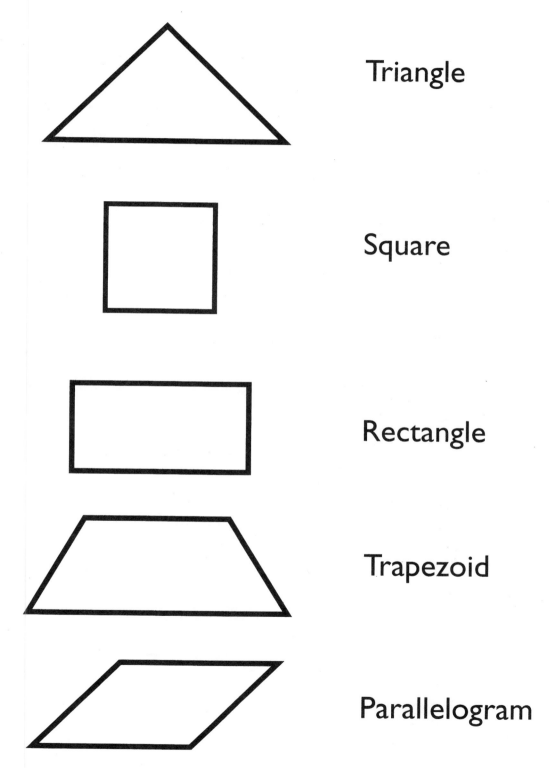

Triangle

Square

Rectangle

Trapezoid

Parallelogram

Making "Build It! Festival"
A School-Wide Event!

Having a school-wide "Build It! Festival" may seem like an ambitious undertaking, and it is, but there is more than enough learning and motivation taking place at a one-time "Build It! Festival" to make it worthwhile for students, teachers, and parents. The Lawrence Hall of Science first presented a school-wide "Build It! Festival" to large groups, up to 150 people at a time. Sometimes, this has been done for students during the school day or in the evenings for a back-to-school night or family math night event.

There are at least two different models for presenting a "Build It! Festival" to large numbers of people: the **large-room** model, where a large group of people interact in an unstructured way at a variety of learning stations, and the **multiple-room** model, in which distinct activities are conducted in separate rooms, and small groups rotate through these rooms on a schedule.

Large-Room Model

The key to conducting a successful "Build It! Festival" for up to 120 people at a time is having enough stations, at least one adult volunteer at every station, and a plan for coordinating the event.

How many stations are enough? That depends. If you have 120 kids participating during one session, you will need enough stations, with enough room at each station, so every child can fully participate. Since there are eight independent learning activities in this guide, you will need to set up one station for each of the eight activities.

At each station, you need to be sure that there are enough materials so at least eight pairs of students can work at any given time. (This means that at any one station you can have 16 kids working. With eight distinct stations and 16 kids working at each station, you can accommodate up to $(16)(8) = 128$ kids.) You will need 8 large (cafeteria size) tables to spread out the materials and directions, as well as a large floor space for the soon-to-be-created Dowel Designs structures. Spread the tables out leaving enough room for the participants to move around freely.

To aid in having a smooth-running "Build It! Festival," it is important to have at least one adult volunteer at each station. Some stations could even use more than one adult—Dowel Designs is one of those stations. It tends to be a popular station and well-visited by participants. Not only should your adult volunteers arrive early to investigate their chosen station, they could help set up as well.

To set up eight stations with enough materials for each station is in itself an arduous task. However, one way of coordinating such an event is to have teachers, or teams of teachers, each be responsible for one station and the necessary materials. Again, make sure there is at least one adult volunteer for each station. Collaboration is not only helpful but may assist in diffusing any anxiety about putting on such a production.

Multiple-Room/ Scheduled Rotation Model

If having enough space is a problem, you may want to consider spreading out the festival. Classes of students can rotate through different classrooms on a schedule, while teachers stay put presenting the same activities each time. These can include the learning stations or any of the "Going Further" activities included in this guide.

While there is certainly effort in planning the event this way, there is a great deal of time savings involved. Each teacher only has to prepare and present one set of activities, and yet their students can experience them all. If done as an evening event, it will prove to be fun for all!

Behind the Scenes
Geometric Glossary

The following geometric glossary provides information that may be helpful to you in answering student questions, planning, gaining some background, and, in general, refreshing your basic knowledge of geometry and its terminology. This section is absolutely NOT meant to be read out loud to students, or duplicated for them. Their direct experience with the activities, rather than vocabulary words or the expression of more abstract concepts, is what *Build It! Festival* is all about!

Introduction

Geometry is the study of lines, angles, shapes, and relationships. As such, it is everpresent in our everyday lives. For example, food items come in a variety of shapes and the relationship between their shapes has an impact on how they can best be stored in a limited space, such as a cabinet or shelf. Street signs are made in different shapes, railroad tracks illustrate a set of parallel lines, both housing construction and interior decoration make use of repeated shapes and interrelated shapes and structures.

Young children's first experience with geometry involves playing with objects in their physical world. Through that experience they develop a vocabulary for common geometric shapes and learn to identify each one. Usually, children begin with two-dimensional shapes (circles, polygons) and then explore three-dimensional ones (cones, rectangular prisms). Included in their explorations is the structure of three-dimensional things such as bridges and buildings as well as other topics in geometry such as symmetry (fold a shape in half and both sides match exactly), reflection (mirror image), and tessellations (patterned tilings).

The following list of geometric terms is designed to provide accurate names for shapes and geometric relationships. ***There is more information contained in this section than is needed to present the "Build It! Festival."***

Points and Lines

A *point* is an element that has no dimension (no size, shape, or extension) and is represented by a dot and labeled with a capital letter.

A *straight line* is often described as the shortest distance between two points and continues forever in both directions. A line contains an infinite number of points and is named by any two points on the line. Two points determine a unique line.

A *ray* has a beginning point and no endpoint. A ray is labeled by its endpoint and any other point on the ray.

A *vertical line* goes straight up and down; it is at a 90° angle to a horizontal line. Telephone poles are examples of vertical line segments.

A *horizontal line* is a line parallel to the plane of the horizon.

Parallel lines are lines that remain an exact distance apart and will never intersect (cross). Train tracks are a real-world example of parallel lines.

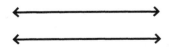

Perpendicular lines are formed by two lines meeting at a 90° angle.

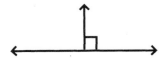

Build It! **Architect/Builder Connection:** As architects describe how to make a structure for the builder, these terms are useful in giving directions.

Angles

An *angle* is formed by two rays with a common endpoint. The amount of difference between the lines is measured in degrees and has special names, depending upon the measure of degrees, as follows:

- *right* angles measure 90°

- *acute* angles measure less than 90°

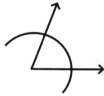

- *obtuse* angles measure more than 90° but less than 180°

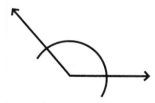

- *straight* angles measure 180°

A *vertex* (plural vertices) is the point of intersection of the two sides of an angle. Examples include a corner of a cube, or of other geometric figure bounded by lines, planes, or lines and planes.

Two-Dimensional Shapes

Plane geometry is the study of shapes and figures in two dimensions—the plane. Plane figures have only length and width.

Circles

A *circle* is a plane figure bounded by a single curved line, every point of which is equally distant from the point at the center of the figure. Circles are named by the letter of their centerpoint. The radius is the distance from the point in the center of the circle to any point along the curved line. The diameter is a line segment passing through the center of the circle from one point on the curved line to another point on the opposite side.

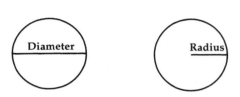

Triangles

A *triangle* is a plane figure with three sides and three angles. The sum of all three angles in any triangle equals 180°.

An *equilateral triangle* has all three sides equal in length and all three angles equal in degrees (60°).

An *isosceles triangle* has two sides of equal length and two angles of equal degrees.

A *right triangle* has one 90° angle.

An *acute triangle* is a triangle with all acute angles (less than 90°).

An *obtuse triangle* is a triangle with one obtuse (more than 90° and less than 180°) angle.

A *scalene triangle* is a triangle with no two equal sides.

Build It! Pattern Block Connection: The green triangle in the pattern block set is an equilateral triangle, as well as an equiangular triangle (all its angles are of equal degrees).

Polygons

A *polygon* is any closed plane figure with three or more sides. "Poly" means many and "gon" means sides, so the word polygon means many sides. A *regular polygon* has all sides and all angles equal. Often polygons that have more than four sides are portrayed as regular polygons.

Quadrilaterals

Any closed figure with four sides and four angles is a quadrilateral. The sum of the angles in any quadrilateral equals 360°. Examples of quadrilaterals include:

A *parallelogram* is a plane figure having the opposite sides parallel and equal in length.

A *rectangle* is a plane figure with 90° angles and opposite sides that are parallel and equal in length.

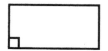

A *rhombus* is a parallelogram with equal sides and opposite angles that are equal in measure.

A *square* is a quadrilateral with all sides of equal length and all angles of 90°. A square is also a rhombus.

A *trapezoid* is a plane figure with only one pair of parallel lines.

Build It! **Pattern Block Connection:** The blue and the tan shapes in the pattern block set are both parallelograms and rhombuses (or rhombi); they are commonly referred to as diamonds. The orange square is also a rectangle and a rhombus. The red shape is a trapezoid.

Other Polygons

A *pentagon* is a closed plane figure with five sides.

A *hexagon* is a closed plane figure with six sides.

A *heptagon* is a closed plane figure with seven sides.

An *octagon* is a closed plane figure with eight sides. A stop sign is an example of a hexagon.

*Polygons that have sides of equal length and angles of equal measure are called **regular polygons**. Often polygons with more than four sides are portrayed as regular polygons. However, all polygons are defined by their number of sides regardless of the length of their sides or measure of their angles. For example, any closed shape with five sides is a pentagon, as any closed shape with six sides is a hexagon, and so on.*

A *nonegon* is a closed plane figure with nine sides.

A *decagon* is a closed plane figure with ten sides.

A *dodecagon* is a closed plane figure with twelve sides.

Polygons can increase to have any number of sides. An *n-gon* is a polygon with *n* number of sides.

Build It! **Fill-A-Shape Connection**: There are two hexagons to fill in this activity and, although only one is regular, they are both hexagons! Similarly there are two dodecagons—count the sides on each! The "shape" does not determine the classification of the shape, the number of sides does!

Build It! **Tangram Connection**: As students build new shapes with the seven tangram shapes they will create a variety of polygons. This list will help identify the names of the less common shapes.

Three-Dimensional Shapes

Three-dimensional shapes are figures that have length, width, and thickness.

A *polyhedron* (the plural is polyhedra or polyhedrons) is a three-dimensional closed figure that is formed by polygonal surfaces. Each polygonal surface is called a *face*. Pairs of faces intersect at *edges*. Three or more edges intersect at a *vertex* (plural vertices). Real world examples of polyhedra include boxes of all shapes and sizes, soup cans, a golf ball, etc.

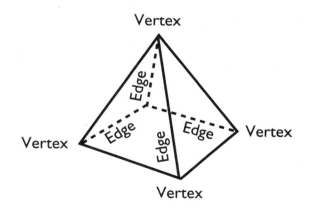

Look at this pyramid. It has four triangular faces (flat polygons) and one square face as a base. The line where two of the triangles meet is an edge. The point at the top is a vertex since four edges intersect at that point.

A *regular polyhedron* is one in which all the polygons formed are congruent (equal in shape and size) to one another.

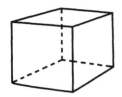

A *prism* is a special type of polyhedron. The following three things must be true for a polyhedron to be a prism:

- two opposite faces (called bases) are congruent polygons (equal in size and shape) that are in parallel planes;

- the faces that are not bases are parallelograms; and

- the edges where the parallelograms intersect are parallel.

A cube and a rectangular box are both examples of prisms.

A *tetrahedron* is a polyhedron with four triangular faces.

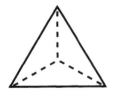

A *pyramid* is a polyhedron with a polygon for a base and triangular faces that meet at a common vertex. The most common pyramid has a square for a base and four equilateral triangles that meet at a vertex.

Get Connected – Free!

Get the *GEMS Network News*,

our free educational newsletter filled with...

- **updates** on GEMS activities and publications
- **suggestions** from GEMS enthusiasts around the country
- **strategies** to help you and your students succeed
- **information** about workshops and leadership training
- **announcements** of new publications and resources

Be part of a growing national network of people who are committed to activity-based math and science education. Stay connected with the **GEMS** **Network News.** *If you don't already receive the* **Network News,** *simply return the attached postage-paid card.*

For more information about GEMS call (510) 642-7771, or write to us at GEMS, Lawrence Hall of Science, University of California, Berkeley, CA 94720-5200, or gems@uclink.berkeley.edu.

Please visit our web site at www.lhsgems.org.

GEMS activities are effective and easy to use. They engage students in cooperative, hands-on, minds-on math and science explorations, while introducing key principles and concepts.

More than 70 GEMS Teacher's Guides and Handbooks have been developed at the Lawrence Hall of Science — the public science center at the University of California at Berkeley — and tested in thousands of classrooms nationwide. There are many more to come — along with local GEMS Workshops and GEMS Centers and Network Sites springing up across the nation to provide support, training, and resources for you and your colleagues!

Yes!

Sign me up for a free subscription to the

GEMS Network News

filled with ideas, information, and strategies that lead to
Great Explorations in Math and Science!

Name_____

Address_____

City_____ State_____ Zip_____

How did you find out about GEMS? (Check all that apply.)
❏ word of mouth ❏ conference ❏ ad ❏ workshop ❏ other: _____
❏ In addition to the *GEMS Network News*, please send me a free catalog of GEMS materials.
❏ Also, sign me up for the online edition of the *GEMS Network News* at this
e-mail address:_____

GEMS
Lawrence Hall of Science
University of California
Berkeley, CA 94720-5200
(510) 642-7771

Ideas ◄
Suggestions ◄
Resources ◄

that lead to Great Explorations
in Math and Science!

101 LAWRENCE HALL OF SCIENCE # 5200

1-61571-25775-62-X

BUSINESS REPLY MAIL
FIRST-CLASS MAIL   PERMIT NO 7   BERKELEY CA

POSTAGE WILL BE PAID BY ADDRESSEE

UNIVERSITY OF CALIFORNIA BERKELEY
GEMS
LAWRENCE HALL OF SCIENCE
PO BOX 16000
BERKELEY CA 94701-9700

NO POSTAGE
NECESSARY
IF MAILED
IN THE
UNITED STATES

Get Connected!

www.lhsgems.org

A *cube* (hexahedron) is a polyhedron with six congruent square faces.

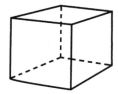

An *octahedron* is a polyhedron with eight polygon faces. A regular octahedron can be constructed with eight equilateral triangular faces.

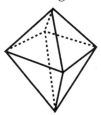

A *dodecahedron* is a polyhedron with twelve polygon faces. A regular dodecahedron can be constructed with twelve regular pentagons.

An *icosahedron* is a polyhedron with twenty polygon surfaces. A regular icosahedron has twenty triangular faces.

   ***Build It!* Connections**: Three-dimensional geometry is explored in three activities in this guide: Create-A-Shape, Dowel Designs, and Polyhedra. Once again, please note that the information in this section is to assist you in naming, classifying, and discussing solid geometric figures and their parts. It is *not* intended as a teaching tool or to be duplicated for or read to students. Use the information as appropriate for your students.

Special Note on Tessellations

Tessellations connect mathematics, history, and art. Starting as early as 4000 B.C., Sumerians created geometric mosaics for decorations. Archimedes (287–212 B.C.) investigated properties of regular polygons that tessellated in the plane.

Probably the most extensive work with mosaic designs was done by the Moorish artists in Spain from 700–1500. These artists developed tessellating geometric patterns (as well as calligraphy) for ornamentation and are especially known for intricate star designs.

Starting in 1930, the Dutch artist, M.C. Escher, began altering geometric shapes and creating tessellating forms such as birds, reptiles, fish, and people. The Escher design on this page is but one of many extraordinary examples.

Many modern artists and interior designers have continued the tessellating tradition, and the increasing sophistication of computer graphics has opened up even more possibilities. Geometric shapes can be translated, rotated, and reflected to create more unusual tessellations. The GEMS Exhibit Guide *Shapes, Loops & Images* provides set-up instructions for a table-top exhibit on tessellations.

Dodecagon Shape Masters

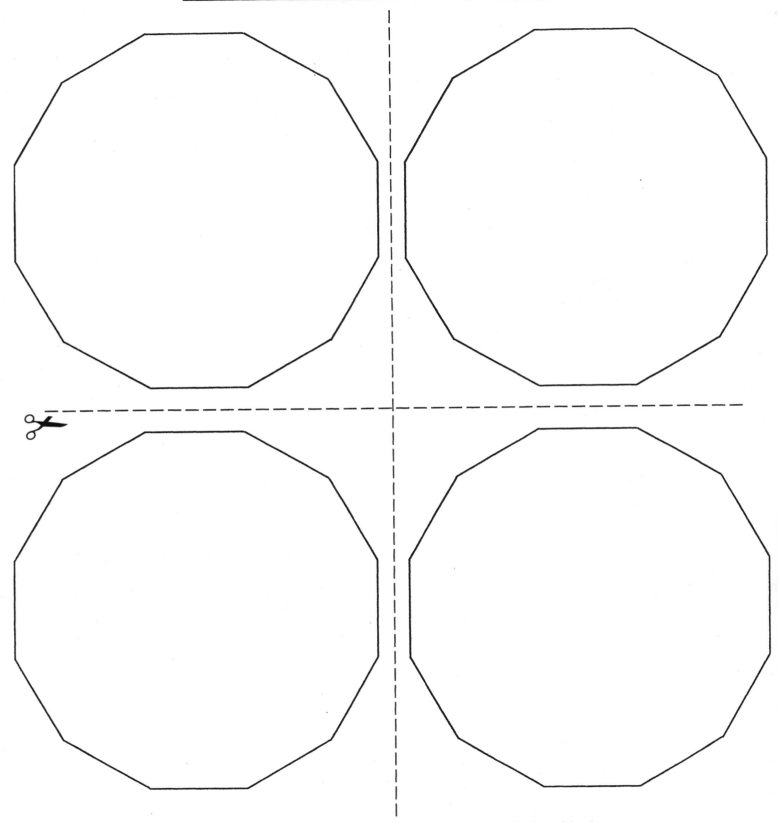

Resource Books

Build It With Boxes by Joan Irvine.
William Morrow and Company, Inc., New York, 1993.

Creating Escher-Type Drawings by E.R. Ranucci and J.L. Teeters.
Creative Publications, Palo Alto, California, 1977.

Exploring With Polydrons (Grades 3–9) by Marilyn Komarc and Gwen Clay.
Books 1 & 2. Cuisenaire Company of America, Inc., White Plains, New York, 1991.

Fractions with Pattern Blocks by Mathew E. Zullie.
Creative Publications, Sunnyvale, California, 1975.

Introduction to Tessellations by Dale Seymour and Jill Britton.
Dale Seymour Publications, Palo Alto, California, 1989.

Kite Craft by Lee Scott Newman and Jay Hartley Newman.
Crown Publishers, New York, 1974.

The Master Revealed—A Journal with Tangrams by Barbara E. Ford.
Tandora's Box Press, Vallejo, California, 1988.

Mathematics Their Way by Mary Baratta Lorton.
Addison-Wesley Publishing Company, Menlo Park, California, 1976.

The Paper Airplane Book by Seymour Simon; illustrated by Byron Barton.
Viking Press, New York, 1971.

Pattern Block Activities by Marian Pasternak and Linda Silvey.
Creative Publications, Sunnyvale, California, 1975.

Polyhedraville by the Beyond Activities Project.
Creative Publications, Mountainview, California, 1994.

Presto Chango by Anne Linehan.
Watten/Poe Teaching Resource Center, San Leandro, California, 1994.

Tangram Treasury by Jan Fair.
Cuisenaire Company of America, Inc., New Rochelle, New York, 1987.

Tessellation Teaching Masters by Dale Seymour.
Dale Seymour Publications, Palo Alto, California, 1989.

Windows to Tangrams: Reproducible Activities, Grades 4–6 by Sue Mogard
and Marilyn Trow. American Teaching Aids, Minneapolis, Minnesota, 1992

Wings & Things by Stephen Weiss; illustrated by Paul Jackson.
St. Martin's Press, New York, 1984.

Please see "Literature Connections," on page 207, for more useful books and for annotations of several of the above. The GEMS Project welcomes your suggestions of useful resource books, literature connections, and any other related resources that you've found to be particularly valuable in exploring geometry and its real world connections. Let us hear from you!

Literature Connections

Anno's Math Games III
by Mitsumasa Anno
Philomel Books/Putnam & Grosset, New York. 1991
Grades: 4–10

Picture puzzles, games, and simple activities introduce the mathematical concepts of abstract thinking, circuitry, geometry, and topology. The book invites active participation. An exploration of triangles includes origami shapes, while a section on ever-popular mazes encourages logical thinking.

Block City
by Robert Louis Stevenson; illustrated by Ashley Wolff
Andersen Press, London. 1988
Grades: K–2

Robert Louis Stevenson's poem "Block City" comes alive for young children through vibrant illustrations. Encourages imaginative building with blocks. Nice classic poetic connection to pattern block and other construction activities.

Bridges
by Ken Robbins
Dial Books, New York. 1991
Grades: K–5

From delicate webs of steel spanning a vast river to stone arches reaching over a highway, bridges expand our world by joining one place with another. This book of hand-tinted photographs of bridges includes many types with descriptions of their design and use.

Castle
by David Macaulay
Houghton Mifflin, Boston. 1977
Grades: K–6

One of a number of outstanding and beautifully illustrated books that focus on human structures, the work of building, architecture, shapes, and related content. Any and all of these books make a great connection to *Build It! Festival*. Other David Macaulay books in this category, with the same publisher, in the K–6 grade range are: *Cathedral* (1973); *City* (1974); *Pyramid* (1975); and *Unbuilding* (1980).

Building An Igloo
by Ulli Steltzer.
Groundwood/Douglas & McIntyre Ltd., Toronto. 1981
Grades: K–5

An Inuit father and son build an igloo to serve as a hunting shelter. The power, beauty and geometry of constructing the igloo are beautifully illustrated in black-and-white photographs. This book is an inspiring real-world connection to the three-dimensional activities in *Build It! Festival*.

Eight Hands Round: A Patchwork Alphabet
by Ann Whitford Paul; illustrated by Jeanette Winter
HarperCollins Publishers, New York. 1991
Grades: 2–6

> This book Introduces the letters of the alphabet with names of early
> American patchwork quilt patterns and describes the activity or
> occupation from which the patterns originate. Another quilt book by the
> same author, *The Season's Sewn: A Year in Patchwork* highlights quilt
> patterns that reflect during the nineteenth century. The designs in both
> books are rich in geometric patterns.

From Blueprint to House
by Franz Högner
Carolrhoda Books, Minneapolis, 1986
Grades: K–2

> This "start to finish" book begins with a blueprint and ends with a com-
> pleted home.

A Grain of Rice
by Helena C. Pittman
Bantam Books, New York. 1992
Grades: 2–5

> A hard-working farmer's son wins the hand of the Emperor's daughter
> through clever use of mathematical knowledge about what results when a
> grain of rice is doubled every day for 100 days. Connects to What Comes
> Next? activity and is an excellent literary introduction to the concept of
> exponential growth.

Grandfather Tang's Story: A Tale Told with Tangrams
by Ann Tompert; illustrated by Robert A. Parker
Crown, New York. 1990
Grades: K–5

> Grandfather tells Little Soo a story about shape-changing fox fairies who
> try to outdo each other until a hunter brings danger to both of them. The
> seven shapes that grandfather uses to tell the story are the pieces of an
> ancient Chinese puzzle, a tangram. Students can make their own
> tangrams, replicating the animals in the story or creating their own. This
> book is a wonderful and powerful way to connect mathematics to literature
> because in itself it embodies the connection, and because creating and
> solving tangrams is an involving activity for all ages.

The Greedy Triangle
by Marilyn Burns; illustrated by Gordon Silveria
Scholastic Inc., New York. 1994.
Grades: K–5

> Dissatisfied with its three sides and three angles, a triangle goes to the
> local shape-shifter to ask for more of each. The first transformation into a
> quadrilateral doesn't satisfy the former triangle. With subsequent visits to
> the shape-shifter, it becomes a pentagon, a hexagon, heptagon, and so on,
> until it finally discovers that being a triangle was really best of all. The
> bright cartoon-like illustrations are filled with examples of where each
> shape can be found in our world.

If You Look Around You
by Fulvio Testa
Dial Books for Young Readers/E.P. Dutton, New York. 1983
Grades: K–3

Geometric shapes (two-dimensional and three-dimensional), points, and lines and depicted in scenes of children in- and out-of-doors. Nice real-world connections to geometry.

The Keeping Quilt
by Patricia Polacco
Simon & Schuster, New York. 1988
Grades: K–5

A homemade quilt ties together the lives of four generations of an immigrant Jewish family, remaining a symbol of their enduring love and faith. Strongly moving text and pictures. A resource to begin a quilt project. Quilts are creative real-life examples of fitting shapes into a defined space, including tessellations, the intriguing mathematical and creative art of *exactly* fitting similar shapes into a defined space. Sidney Taylor Award winner.

The King's Chessboard
by David Birch; illustrated by Devis Grebu
Dial Books, New York. 1988
Grades: K–6

A proud king learns a valuable (and exponential) lesson when he grants his wise man a request for rice that doubles with each day and square on the chessboard. Connects to What Comes Next? activity and, more generally to the mathematics strands of number, pattern, and function.

Kite Craft
by Lee Scott Newman and Jay Hartley Newman
Crown Publishers, New York. 1974
Adult Reference

A comprehensive book about the history and processes of kitemaking throughout the world. Includes sections on the aerodynamics of kites as well as on basic construction techniques.

My Cat Likes to Hide in Boxes
by Eve Sutton; illustrated by Lynley Dodd
Scholastic, New York. 1973
Grades: K–2

Delightful book with rhymes about cats all over the world and "my cat" who likes to hide in boxes! The predictable pattern encourages reading participation. The idea of boxes and using shapes as homes is an early connection to structure and geometry.

Opt: An Illusionary Tale
by Arline and Joseph Baum
Viking Penguin, New York. 1987
Grades: 2–6

> A magical tale of optical illusions in which objects seem to shift color and size while images appear and disappear. You are an active participant in this book as you are guided through the land of Opt. Included are explanations of the illusions and information to assist readers in making their own illusions!

The Paper Airplane Book
by Seymour Simon; illustrated by Byron Barton
Viking Press, New York. 1971
Grades: 3–6

> A user-friendly book on the aerodynamics of airplanes, complete with instructions on how to construct paper airplanes. Emphasis on the structure of airplanes and how changes in structure/shape impact the forces in flight. Additional experiments are included.

The Patchwork Quilt
by Valerie Flournoy; illustrated by Jerry Pinkney
Dial Books, New York. 1985
Grades: K–5

> Using scraps cut from the family's old clothing, Tanya helps her grandmother piece together a quilt of memories. When Grandma becomes ill, Tanya's family also gets involved in the project and they work together to complete the quilt. Quilts, like geometry, are fascinating explorations of shapes and how they fit together.

The Phantom Tollbooth
by Norton Juster; illustrated by Jules Feiffer
Random House, New York. 1989
Grades: 2–8

> Milo has mysterious and magical adventures when he drives his car past The Phantom Tollbooth and discovers The Lands Beyond. On his journey, Milo encounters amusing situations that involve numbers, geometry, measurement, and problem solving. The play on words in the text is delightful.

Round Trip
by Ann Jonas
Greenwillow Books/William Morrow, New York. 1983
Grades: K–3

> Illustrated solely in black and white, this story of a trip between the city and the country is read at first in the standard way, then, on reaching the end, the book is flipped over as the story continues. Lo and behold, the illustrations turned upside down are transformed to depict the new scenes of the story. The strong black/white contrast helps provide a startling demonstration of the ways shapes and images fit into each other and can change, depending on one's perspective.

Rubber Bands, Baseballs and Doughnuts: A Book about Topology
by Robert Froman; illustrated by Harvey Weiss
Thomas Y. Crowell, New York. 1972
Out of print
Grades: 4–8

> An introduction into the world of topology through active reader participation. The activities provide concrete examples and insights into abstract concepts.

Sadako and the Thousand Paper Cranes
by Eleanor Coerr; illustrated by Ronald Himler
Dell Books, New York. 1977
Grades: 3–6

> In this true story a young Japanese girl is dying of leukemia as a result of radiation from the bombing of Hiroshima. According to Japanese tradition, if she can fold 1,000 paper cranes, the gods will grant her wish and make her well, but she was able to fold only 644 paper cranes before she died. In her honor, a Folded Crane Club was organized and each year on August 6, members place thousands of cranes beneath her statue to celebrate Peace Day. The moving story can introduce a class origami project to make 1,000 cranes or other origami figures, and of course connects strongly to social studies and current events issues.

The Secret Birthday Message
by Eric Carle
Harper & Row, New York. 1986
Grades: Preschool–2

> Instead of a birthday package, Tim gets a mysterious letter written in code. Full-color pages, designed with cut-out shapes, allow children to fully participate in this enticing adventure. This book could serve as an exciting way to launch a series of lessons on shapes, which could also include student projects of making "shape books."

Shadowgraphs Anyone Can Make
by Phila H. Webb and Jane Corby
Running Press, Philadelphia. 1991
Grades: K–6

> Illustrates how to make shadowgraphs of various animals and humans. A simple verse accompanies each shadowgraph. Students can create shadows and experiment with the size of these shapes by holding hands nearer or farther from the light.

The Shapes Game
by Paul Rogers; illustrated Stan Tucker
Henry Holt & Co., New York. 1989
Grades: Preschool–2

> Fun-to-say riddles and pictures that are kaleidoscopes of brilliant colors take young children from simple squares and circles through triangles, ovals, crescents, rectangles, diamonds, spirals, and stars.

Shapes, Shapes, Shapes
by Tana Hoban
Greenwillow Books/William Morrow, New York. 1986
Grades: Preschool–5

> Color photographs of familiar objects, such as a chair, barrettes, and a manhole cover, are a way to study round and angular shapes.

Spaces, Shapes and Sizes
by Jane J. Srivastava; illustrated by Loretta Lustig
Thomas Y. Crowell, New York. 1980
Grades: 1–6

> This inviting and well-presented nonfiction book about volume shows the changing forms and shapes a constant amount of sand can take. The book includes estimation activities, an investigation of volume of boxes using popcorn, and a displacement activity. The reader will want to try the activities listed.

The Tipi: A Center of Native American Life
by David and Charlotte Yue
Alfred A. Knopf, New York. 1984
Grades: 5–8

> This excellent book describes not only the structure and uses of tipis, but Plains Indian social and cultural life as well. Some of the cultural language and oversimplification are less vital than they might be, but it is written in an accessible style. There are good charts, exact measurements, and information on the advantages of the cone shape. The central role played by women in constructing the tipi and in owning it are discussed. While this book includes some mention of the negative consequences of European conquest, noting that in some places tipis were outlawed, it is weak in this important area, and should be supplemented with other books.

The Village of Round and Square Houses
by Ann Grifalconi
Little, Brown & Company, Boston. 1986
Grades: K–4

> A grandmother explains to her listeners why the men live in square houses and the women live in round ones in their African village on the side of a volcano. The village of Tos really exists in the remote hills of the Cameroons. This book can begin an exploration of shape and structure. Caldecott Honor book.

Wings & Things
by Stephen Weiss; illustrated by Paul Jackson
St. Martin's Press, New York. 1984
Adult reference

> Contains more than thirty origami models that fly, made from squares or from an 8 ½" x 11" sheet of paper. A great variety of shapes and flight patterns is especially appealing.

Sources for Materials

Pattern Blocks

Please note: Prices given below are to give you an approximate idea of costs of various materials, depending on quantities and which activities you plan to present. The prices and other information were accurate as of the revision of this guide in 2004, but are of course subject to change over time by the distributors involved. Please check with them directly to clarify details and verify prices. We have tried to provide several distributors in most cases. There are of course many other sources for these materials, and we welcome your suggestions.

Small Wooden Pattern Blocks

Pattern blocks are used in four of the activities and for the two preliminary activities. They are invaluable for classroom use. We recommend that for a class of 32 students you purchase six sets. A set consists of 250 wooden pattern blocks including 25 yellow hexagons, 25 orange squares, 50 green triangles, 50 red trapezoids, 50 blue parallelograms, and 50 tan parallelograms.

ETA/Cuisenaire
620 Lakeview Parkway
Vernon Hills, IL 60061
FAX: 800-875-9643
Phone: 800-445-5985
http://www.etacuisenaire.com
- Set of 250 wooden pattern blocks in a lidded storage bucket
$23.95   Item # IN449

Didax Educational Resources
395 Main Street
Rowley, MA 01969   (800) 458-0024
http://www.didaxinc.com
- Set of 250 wooden pattern blocks
$19.95   Item # 2-410

Lakeshore Learning Materials
2695 E. Dominguez Street
P.O. Box 6261
Carson, CA 90749   (800) 421-5354
http://www.Lakeshorelearning.com
- Set of 250 wooden pattern blocks in a lidded storage tub
$19.95   Item # DA334

The Math Learning Center
P.O. Box 3226
Salem, OR 97302   (503) 370-8130
FAX (503) 370-7961
http://www.mlc.pdx.edu
- Set of 250 wooden blocks
$18.00   Item PB

Rainbow Pattern Blocks

The classic pattern block shapes in six brilliant colors. Set includes 432 plastic blocks. These pattern blocks are wonderful for all of the pattern block activities, especially the Tessellations and Symmetry activities.

Math Learning Center
P.O. Box 3226
Salem, OR 97302   (503) 370-8130
FAX: (503) 370-7961
http://www.mlc.pdx.edu
- Set of 250 pieces $18.00

Giant Pattern Block Floor Tiles

Set of 120 large pattern block shapes made out of carpet tiles. The hexagons are 7" and the square is 4" in length.

Didax Educational Resources
395 Main Street
Rowley, MA 01969   (800) 458-0024
- Giant Pattern Block Floor Tiles
  $81.95   Item # 7-GS1

Pattern Block Stickers

Reusable plastic stickers with adhesive backs that match pattern block colors and shapes.

ETA/Cuisenaire
620 Lakeview Parkway
Vernon Hills, Il 60061   (800) 445-9643
FAX: (800) 875-9643
http://www.etacuisenaire.com
$9.95   Item # IN034815